AMERICA the BEAUTIFUL

NEVADA

By Dee Lillegard and Wayne Stoker

Consultants

Phillip I. Earl, Curator of History, Nevada Historical Society

David W. Toll, Author of *The Compleat Nevada Traveler*

Robert L. Hillerich, Ph.D., Bowling Green State University, Bowling Green, Ohio

CHILDRENS PRESS
CHICAGO

The Santa Rosa Range, in north-central Nevada

Project Editor: Joan Downing
Associate Editor: Shari Joffe
Design Director: Margrit Fiddle
Typesetting: Graphic Connections, Inc.
Engraving: Liberty Photoengraving

Library of Congress Cataloging-in-Publication Data

Lillegard, Dee.
   America the beautiful. Nevada / by Dee Lillegard
and Wayne Stoker.
      p.   cm.
   Includes index.
   Summary: Discusses the geography, history,
people, government, economy, and recreation of
Nevada.
   ISBN 0-516-00474-3
   1. Nevada—Juvenile literature. [1. Nevada]
I. Stoker, Wayne. II. Title.
F841.3.L55 1990   90-34665
979.3—dc20   CIP
                                               AC

The First Interstate Bank Tower in Las Vegas

TABLE OF CONTENTS

Chapter 1
THE SILVER STATE

THE SILVER STATE

The gold rushers of 1849 couldn't get through Nevada fast enough on their way to the California goldfields. Few of the forty-niners cared to linger in the scorching deserts and forbidding mountains that separated them from their dream of easy riches. Then there was "that blasted blue stuff" that made Nevada's gold so hard to mine. But in 1859, the blue stuff was discovered to be the purest of silver ore. The fabulous Comstock Lode caused a human stampede back to the land the miners had once spurned.

Treasure hunters came from all over the world, and Nevada challenged them for every ounce of its riches. Only the hardy and the adventuresome could endure in the rugged terrain. The people who stayed in Nevada had to be as rough as the land itself and willing to gamble their lives on the chance of finding a fortune. Boomtowns sprang up by the dozens. When the mines died out, the towns died with them. But the immense wealth of the territory drew more and more settlers, and almost overnight, it seemed, Nevada became the thirty-sixth state.

Today, millions of tourists are drawn to Nevada's resort areas—Las Vegas, the "Entertainment Capital of the World"; Reno, the "Biggest Little City in the World"; and beautiful Lake Tahoe. But for every town in Nevada, there are ten ghost towns—with names such as Rawhide, Seven Troughs, and Silver Reef—and the wide-open spaces of the old frontier remain largely unchanged.

Chapter 2
THE LAND

THE LAND

In his book *Desert Challenge*, Richard Lillard wrote of Nevada,
"From any highway or trail . . . a person can look in any direction
and feel 'as if pretty near all creation were in sight'—a creation
that is vast and colorful and romantic, with purple canyons,
volcanic cliffs of all shades and tints, dark lava flows, creamy
sands, and over all a canopy of blue with puffy white clouds."

GEOGRAPHY AND TOPOGRAPHY

The word *Nevada* means "snowy," or "snow-clad," in Spanish.
The name of the state was taken from the snowcapped Sierra
Nevada, the mountains that first appeared on maps of the region
in the 1600s. Yet most of Nevada is hot, dry desert.

Spread out over 110,540 square miles (286,299 square
kilometers), Nevada ranks seventh in size among the fifty states.
Its greatest distance from north to south, 478 miles (769
kilometers), covers seven degrees of latitude. Nevada is bordered
by five other states: Oregon and Idaho on the north, Utah and
Arizona on the east, and California on the south and west. Most
of the Sierra Nevada lies in California.

Eons ago, the Pacific Ocean covered much of present-day
Nevada. Over many millions of years, mountains rose up above
the ocean surface, only to sink beneath the seas again and again.
Plants and sea animals were swallowed up in the process, creating
great mineral deposits. The mountains and deserts of present-day
Nevada are products of the last million years.

An irrigated field at the foot of Job's Peak in the Sierra Nevada

Most of Nevada lies in what Captain John Charles Frémont, an early explorer and topographer, misnamed the Great Basin. Unlike a deep basin, this vast plateau is 4,000 to 5,000 feet (1,219 to 1,524 meters) above sea level. It comprises an area of 210,000 square miles (543,900 square kilometers) between the Sierra Nevada and the Wasatch Mountains in Utah. The Great Basin is actually a series of 90 basins separated from each other by more than 160 mountain ranges, most of which run in a north-south direction. As seen from above, these mountains have been described as a huge "army of caterpillars crawling toward Mexico."

Nevada's deserts and mountains are the result of powerful earthquakes and volcanic eruptions. Thousands of years of storms, winds, and floods wore down the mountains and created long, wide valleys between them. The process of erosion continues today, with occasional floods carrying tons of debris down from the Sierra to the lower lands. Earthquakes also continue to jolt the state, but, for the most part, they occur in areas where few people live.

RIVERS, LAKES, AND HOT SPOTS

About ten thousand years ago, glaciers covered some of Nevada's mountains. These slow-moving masses of ice and snow gradually melted, producing rivers that swept into the valleys and formed large lakes. The largest, Lake Lahontan, once covered some 8,450 square miles (21,886 square kilometers).

As the weather in the area grew warmer and drier, the vast Lahontan evaporated. Today, the only large remnants of Lahontan are Walker and Pyramid lakes, in the western part of the state.

In 1844, John Frémont named Pyramid Lake after the largest of its unusual rock islands, which reminded him of an ancient Egyptian pyramid. But to the Indians of the region, the island — which towered almost 500 feet (152 meters) above the water — looked like a basket being held over a wicked squaw. The steam rising from hot springs on the island was the squaw's breath coming through the cracks in the basket.

Hot springs can be found in many parts of Nevada. Among the hottest are the Beowawe Geysers in the northeastern part of the state. Unfortunately, by 1980, the high-shooting streams of hot water at Beowawe had been destroyed by vandalism. Even so, the water in the ground is still extremely hot and gives off plenty of steam.

By contrast, Lake Tahoe — in the Sierra Nevada — is cold and glassy blue. It is the largest and second-deepest alpine lake in

Nevada's bodies of water range from steamy hot springs and geysers (left) to the cold, glassy blue waters of Lake Tahoe (above).

North America. Nevada shares beautiful Lake Tahoe, and the forests that surround it, with California.

Nevada's rivers have been described as a "meager lot." In almost any other state, they would be called streams. Lake Tahoe feeds the Truckee River, which winds its way to Pyramid Lake. Like the Truckee, the Carson and Walker rivers also originate in the Sierra. Few of Nevada's rivers make their way to the sea. Most evaporate during the dry season from July to November, leaving behind salty mud flats.

The longest river within the state's borders is the Humboldt, which crosses nearly 300 miles (483 kilometers) of northern Nevada before it empties into Rye Patch Reservoir and then vanishes in a tangle of swamp and salt puddles called the Humboldt Sink. Most of Nevada's rivers die out in smaller desert sinks. The Humboldt earned a particularly bad reputation among early travelers who followed the Humboldt Trail west. One Iowa man wrote a poem about the river that begins: "Meanest and muddiest, filthiest stream/most cordially I hate you. . . ."

The strangest river in the state is the Amargosa, in southern Nevada. Saturated with salts and alkali, the bitter Amargosa travels underground during part of its course before finally disappearing near Death Valley.

The powerful Colorado River runs along the southeastern edge of Nevada. The river was sometimes a muddy torrent, other times a thin stream, until Hoover Dam was built in the 1930s to control it. Shared by Nevada and Arizona, this engineering wonder is more than twice the length of a football field and contains enough concrete to pour a 4-inch- (10-centimeter-) thick, four-lane highway clear across the country. The dam's reservoir, Lake Mead, is the largest man-made reservoir in the United States.

Also taming the Colorado is the smaller Davis Dam, which created Lake Mohave. Other dams and reservoirs in the state help Nevada make the most of its scant water supply.

STRANGE FORMATIONS

Over thousands of years, wind and water have created many unusual formations in Nevada. In the Valley of Fire in Clark County, nature has sculpted eerie shapes out of brilliant red sandstone. In late afternoon, the rays of the sun on the red rock can make the whole valley seem on fire.

Some of the canyons in Nevada's mountains are so steep and deep that the sun's rays hardly touch their floors. At Cathedral Gorge, in Lincoln County, wind and rain have sculpted soft bentonite clay into shapes that resemble cathedral spires, pillars and palaces, dragons and hunchbacked men.

Unusual rock formations, such as those at Cathedral Gorge (left) and the Valley of Fire (right), are part of Nevada's landscape.

In a few places in Nevada, winds have created huge sandpiles. Sand Mountain, near Fallon, is sometimes called the "Singing Mountain" because of the humming sound the breezes make as they drift over the sand.

When John Frémont tried to describe Nevada, he realized it had to be seen to be believed. Even today, to those unfamiliar with it, Nevada's landscape can seem like another planet.

CLIMATE

Nevada's climate varies to extremes, with some of the highest and lowest temperatures in the nation. In snow-covered areas atop the highest mountains in the northeastern part of the state, temperatures often drop to minus 30 degrees Fahrenheit (minus

Though temperatures soar in Nevada's desert areas in the summer (left), the winters can be cool enough to allow snowfall (right).

34 degrees Celsius). In the southern tip of the state, where the desert is near sea level, temperatures climb to the opposite extreme, sometimes reaching 115 to 120 degrees Fahrenheit (46 to 49 degrees Celsius).

Temperatures in Nevada can also vary widely within a single day, sometimes as much as 50 degrees. Cool evenings in the heat of summer and mild days in the cold of winter are not uncommon.

The seasons in Nevada vary from region to region. In the northern and eastern areas, the winters are long and cold and the summers are short and hot. In southern Nevada, however, the summers are long and extremely hot, while the winters are short and mild.

Nevada's annual precipitation averages about 9 inches (23 centimeters), less than any other state. Some areas of Nevada drink in as little as 3 inches (8 centimeters) a year. Most of the state's precipitation occurs in the form of snowfall, which covers not only the pine trees in the mountains, but the sagebrush in the high deserts as well.

THE LAND AND ITS USES

Though Nevada's climate is a challenge to life, a surprising variety of plants and animals have learned to survive in it. In the desert, cactus, yucca, and sagebrush all bloom during short periods of the year, and wildflowers create a carpet of color. Scrub brush gives way to piñon-juniper forests at the edge of the mountainous areas, and at higher altitudes, firs and pines thrive.

The swift-footed mule deer of the mountains and the pronghorn antelope of the valleys are among the few large animals that make Nevada their home. However, legions of small creatures, including jackrabbits, chipmunks, gophers, mice, and many varieties of lizards and snakes, can be found in Nevada. Many kinds of birds—from the tiny hummingbird to the fierce golden eagle—thrive throughout the state. Flocks of migrating ducks and geese cross Nevada, and—strange as it may sound—in the middle of the desert, at Pyramid Lake, white pelicans breed. In fact, Anaho Island, in the middle of Pyramid Lake, is a national wildlife refuge.

As a result of its numerous reclamation and irrigation projects, Nevada has far more usable land today than the early pioneers would have dreamed possible. But the largest part of Nevada—more than 85 percent—is public land owned by the federal government. This land includes Indian reservations, national forests, and military and recreational sites. Ranchers lease the land to graze cattle and sheep; wild horses still roam over it; and backpackers, hunters, and fishermen enjoy its vast wilderness.

The stillness and natural beauty of Nevada's wide-open spaces are among the state's greatest resources. No other state except Alaska has such a large proportion of unspoiled land, and Nevadans want to keep it that way.

Chapter 3
THE
PEOPLE

THE PEOPLE

WHO ARE THE NEVADANS?

Native Americans (American Indians) were Nevada's first residents. In fact, the Nevada region was the home of some of the earliest American Indians. The Paiutes, Shoshones, and Washos were the major Indian groups living in Nevada when European explorers began to arrive in the region in the 1800s. Today, descendants of these groups live on tribal lands throughout the state.

With the discovery of silver in 1859, Europeans and Asians flocked to Nevada, along with Americans from other states. By 1870, nearly half of the state's population was foreign-born. Most of these people were hard workers with high hopes who had come to America to escape poverty.

Irish and Cornish (natives of Cornwall, England) worked deep in the mines of the Comstock Lode; Italians and Swiss burned charcoal for the mine smelters and established ranches and dairies in the valleys near Reno; French Canadians worked as lumberjacks in the forests surrounding Lake Tahoe; Germans farmed in the fertile Carson Valley; Chinese laid railroad tracks across the state. Later, Slavs and Greeks came to eastern Nevada to work in the copper mines and smelters of White Pine County, while Basques (people from the Basque region of Spain) and Scots herded sheep in the deserts and mountains.

Altogether, more than thirty nationalities peopled Nevada. Their languages and customs became an integral part of the state's

A family enjoying the Emerald Bay Overlook at Lake Tahoe

heritage in place names, literature, music, dances, and festivals. The latest waves of immigration into Nevada have come from Mexico and southeast Asia. Hispanic children and the children of Vietnamese refugees make up the largest number of students enrolled in special English-language classes.

In 1988, whites made up more than 80 percent of the state's population. Hispanics comprised 7.2 percent; blacks, 6.5 percent; Asians and Pacific Islanders, 2.7 percent. Though Native Americans are the state's smallest minority group, Nevada ranks among the top ten states in percentage of American Indians.

The two largest religious groups in Nevada are Roman Catholics and Mormons (members of the Church of Jesus Christ of Latter-day Saints). Mormons have moved west from neighboring Utah and established a number of small towns in western Nevada. Though Roman Catholics make up about half of Nevada's church members, Mormons are the fastest-growing religious group in the state. Members of Protestant denominations and a Jewish minority make up the remainder of Nevada's religious adherents.

Nevada has about equal numbers of Democrats and Republicans, but its people deal with issues along conservative lines regardless of party affiliation. The Republican party dominated the presidential popular vote in Nevada throughout the 1970s and 1980s. In the 1980 presidential election—and again, overwhelmingly, in 1984—the majority of Nevadans voted for Republican candidate Ronald Reagan. The general chairman of Reagan's reelection campaign was Reagan's close friend and advisor, Nevada Republican Senator Paul Laxalt. In 1988, 60 percent of Nevada's voters chose Republican George Bush in the national presidential election.

A "TWO-CITY STATE"

Although Nevada is the nation's seventh-largest state, it ranks forty-seventh in population density. On the average, Nevada has 7 people for every square mile (3 people per square kilometer) of land. By contrast, the much smaller state of New Jersey ranks first in population density, averaging 940 people per square mile (363 people per square kilometer). However, Nevada's population density figures are somewhat misleading, for more than 80 percent of Nevada's people actually live on only about 4 percent of its land. Most Nevadans live within a 30-mile (48-kilometer) radius of either Reno or Las Vegas.

In the 1970s, Nevada's population increased 63.8 percent—from 488,738 to 800,493—the fastest growth rate in the nation. In 1986, the state's population was estimated to have finally passed the 1-million mark. Nevada's continuing growth is due largely to the steady immigration of people from other states. Nevada has the lowest percentage of native-born residents of all the states, with those moving into Nevada outnumbering those born in the state by more than four to one.

In contrast to Reno and Las Vegas, some of Nevada's rural towns are so small that, as one traveler commented, "even a ninety-pound weakling could rip the local phone book in half." In northeastern Nevada, the bus goes through the tiny town of Eureka in one direction on Monday and returns—from the other direction—on Friday.

Among the most colorful Nevadans are the Basques, who have maintained the cultural traditions of their European ancestors with little change. Renowned for their feasts and festivals, the Basques have a unique social life centering around home and family.

In Nevada, people traditionally maintain a warm, open-door policy. But Nevadans also respect individual freedom and, as one observer put it, "they mostly leave you alone, no matter who you are."

TRENDS OF THE EIGHTIES

By 1988, Nevada had the second-fastest-growing senior population in the country. Increasing numbers of people over the age of sixty-five find Nevada a desirable place to retire.

For those still busy earning a living, Nevada continues to offer more service jobs than any other state. Those working in hotel, gaming (gambling), and recreation jobs accounted for 44 percent of Nevada's work force in the mid-1980s.

Nevada's people are a diverse lot. Added to this is an array of tourists, equally as diverse, who enjoy the state's entertainment twenty-four hours a day.

Chapter 4
THE BEGINNING

THE BEGINNING

American Indians lived in Nevada thousands of years before the first white men entered the Great Basin scarcely more than two hundred years ago. Like the animals and plants in this harsh environment, the Indians waged a constant struggle to survive. But they came to know the land and its seasons well, and would find a greater threat to their survival in the intruding newcomers.

THE ORIGINAL NEVADANS

Excavations from various archaeological sites around the state indicate that people lived in Nevada as early as twelve thousand years ago. The remains of these people have been found with the bones of extinct horses, camels, and elephants, suggesting that early Nevadans shared the land with large prehistoric animals. In several parts of Nevada, rock hunters have discovered stone dart points that are about ten thousand years old. These darts are typical of a Stone Age culture and were used for hunting before the invention of the bow and arrow.

About three thousand years ago, Lovelock Cave, in the Humboldt Range of northern Nevada, was a favorite dwelling place of some of the early Nevadans. The cave was at that time located on the shore of Lake Lahontan, and the people who inhabited it were talented basket makers. The Lovelock culture was fairly advanced, but for unknown reasons declined about five hundred years ago.

Replicas of Nevada's ancient Indian pueblos are featured at the Lost City Museum in Overton.

From about 500 B.C., a group of people known as the Anasazi
(or "Ancient Ones") lived in simple pit houses in the Moapa
Valley, some 60 miles (97 kilometers) northeast of present-day
Las Vegas. Around A.D. 500, the Anasazi began to mine salt and
turquoise and trade with their neighbors. Their dwellings became
more elaborate, and they made pottery and bows and arrows.

After A.D. 700, the Anasazi built dams on the Virgin and Muddy
rivers and grew cotton, corn, beans, and squash, becoming
Nevada's first farmers. Some of them built adobe pueblos (flat-
roofed clay dwellings). Some of these pueblos had as many as one
hundred chambers. As scores of villages sprang up in the valley, it
became the first large population center of Nevada.

The Anasazi flourished at what is now called Pueblo Grande de
Nevada, or Lost City. (The original city is now covered by the
waters of Lake Mead.) About A.D. 1150, the Anasazi abandoned
their homes and fields without a trace. Their disappearance is a
mystery to archaeologists. Some theorize that these Pueblo people

Four major Indian groups, including the Shoshones (left) and Paiutes
(right), lived in Nevada when white explorers first arrived.

migrated east to Arizona and New Mexico because of drought,
famine, or disease. Another possibility is that they were driven
out by the Paiutes, hunters and gatherers who replaced them.

MODERN NEVADA INDIANS

Some twenty-seven tribal groups existed at one time or another
in Nevada. But only four—the Northern Paiutes, the Southern
Paiutes, the Shoshones, and the Washos—occupied most of
Nevada when the earliest explorers arrived. These Indians knew
nothing about the peoples who had preceded them, and few knew
anything about farming. They were basically hunters, fishermen,
and gatherers, whose desert culture was superbly adapted to their
natural environment.

For the Paiutes, Shoshones, and Washos, life centered around
the family. Within each tribe, small bands had their own

organizations and their own territories. These groups sometimes went their separate ways, making seasonal migrations in search of food. But several times during the year, families or bands came together for rabbit drives and festivals. They feasted, danced, told stories, and played a variety of games.

Tools and household implements made by the early Nevada Indians show their ability to work well with the materials nature gave them, such as stones, grasses, and reeds. All the Indian groups excelled at basket making, but the Washos, who spent their summers in the vicinity of Lake Tahoe, are considered the best. The last of the Washo basket makers was a woman named Dat-So-La-Lee, whose baskets are works of art prized by modern collectors. Dat-So-La-Lee became so famous that the Nevada state legislature passed a law to preserve her work.

The Indians of Nevada were generally not warlike. They believed in a peaceful spirit world where the dead kept watch over the living. They also believed that special powers existed in nature, in the mountains and lakes, in the winds and fog, and in animals. Having no concept of land ownership, they had no idea that men so unlike themselves would lay claim to the land they used and cherished.

THE FIRST EXPLORERS

Nevada as we know it today was part of the territory claimed by Spain when the Spanish conquered Mexico in 1521. However, the Spanish did not enter Nevada for at least another 250 years. In 1776, Father Francisco Garcés may have touched Nevada's southern tip as he searched for a new route from New Mexico to California, thus becoming the first white man to set foot in Nevada.

In 1821, Mexico won its independence from Spain, and Nevada became part of the Mexican territory. Mexico, however, did not seem to think the Nevada region was worth occupying or exploring.

The eastern craze for fur hats and coats led British trappers into Nevada in the late 1820s. In his search for beaver, Peter Skene Ogden, representing the British-owned Hudson's Bay Company, discovered the Humboldt River. (Explorer John Frémont later named the river after German scientist Baron Alexander von Humboldt.)

Jedediah Smith, another fur trapper, was the first American to enter Nevada and the first white man to cross the state. In 1826, Smith led a group of fur trappers westward across the Las Vegas Valley region to California, where they spent the winter. In the spring, the party returned eastward, this time crossing the central Sierra Nevada and the vast desert that became known as the Great Basin. Unaware of the existence of the Humboldt River just to the north, Smith and his men barely survived the journey through the desert. Smith lost his maps and notes, but he had a phenomenal memory and could accurately picture any map or region he had ever seen. Jedediah Smith's findings greatly influenced those who came after him.

Members of the Walker-Bonneville party of 1833-34 became the first white men to follow the Humboldt River west. Joseph Walker was a lieutenant in the trapping expedition of French-born American army officer Benjamin de Bonneville. Walker and about forty men left the main expedition north of the Great Salt Lake and crossed the salt flats of Utah into Nevada.

Near the Humboldt Sink, Walker and his men encountered some eight hundred Northern Paiutes, most of whom had never seen firearms. Hostilities broke out, and the trappers killed thirty

The first accurate mapping of the Nevada region was done by John Frémont, shown here camping at Pyramid Lake (above). One of Frémont's guides was Kit Carson, whose statue now graces the grounds of the Nevada State Capitol (left).

or forty of the Indians. The rest of the Paiutes fled in terror, ending what was Nevada's first large-scale battle between Indians and whites.

From the Humboldt Sink, the Walker party crossed the desert and ran out of food. South of what is now the Walker River, they were reduced to eating dried lake flies. But they went on to forge a path over the Sierra Nevada into California.

The expeditions that followed probably had a secret purpose. In the 1840s, many Americans believed in the concept of "Manifest Destiny," America's right to expand across the continent. Though the United States government officially sent army Lieutenant John Charles Frémont west on a "scientific expedition," he may actually have been sent to survey the territory in hopes of taking it from Mexico. On various expeditions, Frémont was guided by Joseph Walker; Christopher "Kit" Carson, the experienced mountain man; and Truckee, chief of the Northern Paiutes. Frémont's explorations yielded the first truly accurate mapping of the Nevada region.

THE EMIGRANTS

The flood of humanity that was to migrate from the eastern
United States to the Pacific began as a trickle in the early 1840s. In
1841, John Bidwell and John Bartleson led the first successful
emigrant crossing of the Great Basin. From Missouri, the
Bartleson-Bidwell party made its way to the Humboldt River.
Without a map or a guide, the emigrants crossed the Forty-Mile
Desert—a treacherous stretch between the Humboldt, Truckee,
and Carson rivers—and the Sierra Nevada, reaching California
safely after a grueling six months.

Other emigrant parties successfully crossed Nevada between
1841 and 1845. But in October 1846, the Donner party—a group
including men, women, and children—became trapped in the
Sierra by heavy snowfall. When relief finally came to the starving
emigrants, four months later, nearly half of them had died. Some
of the survivors had become so desperate that they ate their dead
comrades. Stories of the Donner party's grisly experience brought
traffic along the Humboldt Trail to a standstill.

Between 1846 and 1848, the United States fought and won the
Mexican War, acquiring the future states of California, Nevada,
and Utah, as well as parts of Arizona, New Mexico, Colorado, and
Wyoming. The discovery of gold in California in 1848 caused a
flood of emigrants west. They came on horseback, by wagon and
buggy, and on foot, following the Humboldt River. Dust-choked,
plagued by hunger and illness, many were forced to abandon their
wagons as their oxen died of starvation.

One group of forty-niners decided to avoid the Humboldt, and
the dreaded Forty-Mile Desert, by going south and following the
Old Spanish Trail. They wandered across the vast, barren Las
Vegas Valley, then into Death Valley, a great, below-sea-level

depression that begins at the southwestern edge of present-day Nevada. It was a miracle that any of them survived to give the region its name.

Most of the emigrants pushed on to California, but some settled in Nevada. In 1850, the United States Congress made most of what is now Nevada a part of the Utah Territory. Mormon leader Brigham Young was appointed territorial governor. A group of Mormons established the first settlement in Nevada, a trading station called Mormon Station near the slopes of the Sierra in Carson Valley. As more people settled in the territory, the Utah legislature created Carson County.

THE COMSTOCK LODE

In 1850, Mormon settlers discovered a few nuggets of gold near the mouth of Gold Canyon. But with all the exciting reports about California, this dusty desert find created little interest.

The few miners who roamed the hills near Gold Canyon panned for gold. By 1858, many of them thought the canyon was played out. But in February 1859, a party of prospectors found a ledge rich in gold at the foot of Sun Mountain (later called Mount Davidson). They had stumbled upon "Gold Hill," part of what was to be the richest mining district in the world, in a region that the Indians called Washoe. Then along came Henry Comstock, known as a "loud-spoken trickster" who was "half-mad." Comstock claimed that the men were on his property. He demanded, and got, a full share in the discovery, and succeeded in giving it his name. In June 1859, two miners, Peter O'Riley and Patrick McLaughlin, began excavating at the Ophir Ravine, not far from Gold Hill, and made another strike.

None of them realized the size or the richness of the Comstock

Westward-bound Mormons in the 1850s

Lode. They cursed the mud that made the gold hard to mine. But when some of this "blasted blue stuff" was analyzed by assayers in California, it was found to be rich in silver. In fact, the mud that the miners had been throwing away was more valuable than the gold. In July 1859, the "rush to Washoe" was on, emptying California's worked-out gold towns.

By November, a lively camp of sagebrush shanties and canvas shacks had sprung up around the Ophir mine. The town was called Pleasant Hill, Ophir, and various other names. But Henry Comstock later told the story of how miner James "Old Virginia" Finney (or Fennimore) was out one night with a lot of the "boys," when he fell down and broke his whiskey bottle. Not wanting to waste his "tarantula juice," Old Virginia christened the settlement *Virginia*, naming it after his home state.

Virginia City was about to become one of the most important cities in the West. But few of the original prospectors got rich. They were soon outnumbered by miners, businessmen, and gamblers from California, who came flocking back over the Sierra to seek their fortunes.

THE PYRAMID LAKE WAR

During the stormy winter of 1859-60, food was scarce. Many of the fortune hunters fell ill and died because of bad water or exposure to the harsh weather. Shootings and brawls were frequent among the hotheaded Comstockers in what was still a barren and lawless part of the Utah Territory.

Within a few months, miners needing fuel stripped the hillsides of the piñon trees, whose nuts the Indians depended upon for food. They slaughtered the Indians' game animals and drove their ponies off the grasslands. Some of the Paiute leaders wanted to make war on the invaders of their land. But Chief Winnemucca, son of Truckee, argued against it.

In May 1860, war became unavoidable when three white men kidnapped two Paiute girls. A handful of Paiutes rescued the women at a trading station on the Carson River, killing their captors and burning the station down. When the story reached Virginia City, 30 miles (48 kilometers) away, more than 100 rowdy Comstockers marched toward the Paiute camp at Pyramid Lake. They walked into an ambush, and 76 of them lost their lives. The frantic inhabitants of Virginia City sought help from the United States Army, and in the second battle of the Pyramid Lake War, nearly 160 Indians were killed. The surviving Indians retreated.

After the conflict, United States Army troops stayed on to build Fort Churchill near the Carson River. A number of military posts were built throughout Nevada during the 1860s to protect the main travel routes and settlements from Indian attack.

Winnemucca is said to have argued with the warlike members of his tribe, "You would make war on the whites. [But they] are like the sands in the bed of your rivers; when taken away they

Paiute Chief Winnemucca (seated at left) and his daughter Sarah (left) worked hard to maintain peace with the white settlers.

only give place for more to come and settle there. . . . They will come like sand in a whirlwind and drive you from your homes." Winnemucca proved to be right.

Virginia City, on the east flank of Mount Davidson, was more than a mile (1.6 kilometers) above sea level and, before 1860, could be reached only by burro. But with the discovery of silver, companies began to build wagon roads up Mount Davidson, using dynamite to blast through solid rock. Workers crawled all over the mountain, creating roads that snaked through canyons, over high passes, and along steep cliffs.

The streets of Virginia City were soon crowded with "prairie schooners," freight wagons drawn by long lines of burros or horses. By the end of the summer of 1860, barely a year after its birth, Virginia City had more than a hundred business establishments, including forty-two saloons, nine restaurants, and ten laundries.

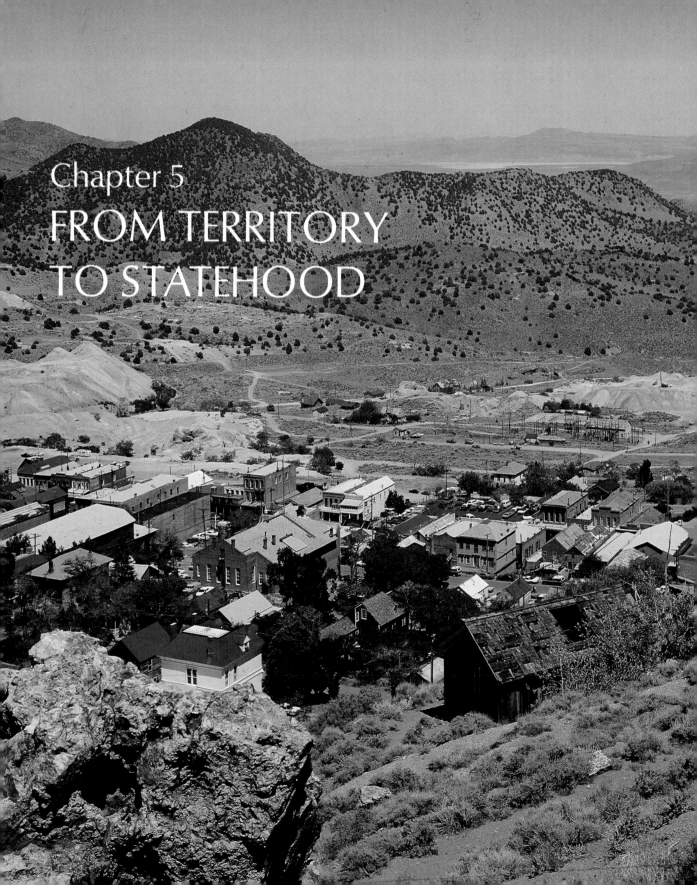

Chapter 5
FROM TERRITORY
TO STATEHOOD

FROM TERRITORY TO STATEHOOD

As the Nevada region yielded its riches and settlements boomed, the eastern half of the United States headed toward civil war. Distant as the silver mines of Nevada seemed from the battlefields of the North and South, the two worlds were inextricably linked.

THE COMSTOCK CHALLENGE

The miners of the Comstock soon faced the problem of reduction—how to refine, or reduce, the ore that contained the gold and silver. The precious minerals had to be separated from worthless rock, and few of the miners knew how to do this.

In August 1859, a four-stamp mill was dragged by oxen over the mountains from Sacramento, California, to the Carson River. The heavy iron stamps soon rose and fell like pile drivers, crushing the ore to be reduced. But this method of reduction was not efficient enough for the anxious miners. Together with the millmen, they began to experiment with new methods.

Mining engineer Almarin B. Paul is generally credited with developing the "Washoe Pan Process." Huge iron pans were used to mix the crushed ore with chemicals that separated the gold and silver. By June 1860, Paul's twenty-four-stamp mill in Gold Canyon was operating so successfully that a mill-building craze followed. Within a few years, some eighty mills operated in and around Virginia City—but there was not enough ore to keep them all busy.

The Comstock Lode, for all its riches, was a miner's nightmare. Instead of one clear vein of ore, its deposits were scattered about like raisins in a pudding. The veins, or ore bodies, were unstable and likely to move or cave in when not properly supported. As the mines descended into the earth, it became harder to mine the ore without causing a cave-in. Many accidents occurred, and miners were killed or injured by falling rocks.

The Ophir miners sought help from Philipp Deidesheimer, a German engineer who had immigrated to California. Deidesheimer developed the basic idea for square-set timbering, a framework that would safely support the walls of the mines while ore was being extracted. With this system, hollow frames of timber were joined in strong interlocking cubes, resembling a honeycomb. The cubes could be extended in any direction, allowing the miners to take ore from above, from ahead, or from either side of them. Eventually, square-set timbering was adopted in mines all over the world.

With the square-set method, the Comstock could now be opened to greater and greater depths. Within a few years, more than a hundred mines tapped the lode. Unfortunately, the square sets required tremendous amounts of timber. The nearest source of wood was the pine forests of the Sierra, and before long, the slopes were stripped of trees for a stretch of nearly 100 miles (161 kilometers).

At first the wood was carried to the mines in huge wagons. But as the lumbermen found themselves working higher and higher up the mountains, a better method of transporting the wood was needed. A rancher named James Haines solved the problem by

Square-set timbering, shown here in a cross-section diagram, kept the walls of a mine from caving in as ore was extracted.

inventing the V-flume, named for its shape. The V-flume floated timber and firewood for miles down the mountains and became standard equipment in western logging.

The miners also had to deal with underground water that poured into the mines. Because western Nevada lies on top of a large thermal belt, this water grew uncomfortably hotter the deeper the miners went. They began using heavy machinery to pump out the water and to hoist the ore from the ever-increasing depths of the mines.

By 1863, Virginia City had a population of more than fifteen thousand. But, as author Mark Twain wrote, there was another busy city beneath it, ". . . down in the bowels of the earth, where a great population of men thronged in and out among the intricate maze of tunnels and drifts, flitting hither and thither under a winking sparkle of lights. . . ."

The Pony Express was a relay race against time; as one rider came into a station, another quickly galloped off.

THE PONY EXPRESS

In March 1860, San Francisco newspapers carried an unusual advertisement:

> YOUNG SKINNY WIRY FELLOWS not over
> eighteen. Must be expert riders willing to risk
> death daily. Orphans preferred.

The Pony Express made its first run on April 3, 1860. Its riders—some only fourteen or fifteen years old—carried important documents between San Francisco and St. Joseph, Missouri. They covered this distance of nearly 2,000 miles (3,219 kilometers) in a record ten days, using the central, or Simpson, route across Nevada.

Fresh horses were ready at relay stations along the route, and riders were given two minutes to change horses. Racing at breakneck speed, a rider's average rate of travel was about 9 miles (14 kilometers) per hour. But at that time, the Pony Express was considered the closest thing to lightning. Danger was constant, whether from the elements or the Indians. Even so, during its eighteen months of existence, the Pony Express lost only one bag of mail.

On October 24, 1861, the transcontinental telegraph was completed, meeting the need for a fast way to communicate information. A message that had taken ten days by Pony Express could now be transmitted by telegraph in ten seconds.

THE BATTLE-BORN STATE

Nevada was no longer just a stretch of barren land to be hurried across. By 1861, its mines were producing millions of dollars a year in silver and gold, and it was well known that Nevada's citizens wanted a government of their own, free from Utah control.

On the other side of the continent, Americans were on the verge of a war between the states. In violent disagreement over the issue of slavery, the southern states had seceded from the Union, creating the Confederate States of America.

The South, concerned about preserving the institution of slavery, had resisted adding any new "free-soil" (nonslave) territories to the Union. But after the southern states seceded, Congress was able to pass a bill creating a separate Nevada Territory. President James Buchanan signed the bill on March 2, 1861, as one of his last acts in office. Two days later, Buchanan's successor, Abraham Lincoln, appointed New York Republican James W. Nye territorial governor of Nevada.

Leaving New York on a luxury ship, Nye started for Nevada with a dozen other officeholders and their aides. Orion Clemens, a lawyer and one-time newspaper publisher in Missouri, had been appointed territorial secretary of the Nevada Territory. His brother Samuel came overland by steamboat and stagecoach to serve as Orion's private secretary. Samuel Clemens would later gain worldwide fame as a writer and humorist, using the pen name Mark Twain.

It took Governor Nye three months to reach the Nevada Territory. William Stewart, a powerful attorney in Carson City, convinced Nye that the territorial capital should be located there. He and some of his friends had real estate interests in and around Carson City. Only a year old, Carson City consisted of a handful of buildings situated around a town square. But it was only a few miles from the Comstock Lode and shared the turbulent life of Virginia City. Nye was installed in Nevada's first governor's mansion, a two-room white frame house. Later, a territorial council—further influenced by Stewart—made Carson City the permanent capital.

Orion Clemens set up the office of territorial secretary in the same room where he slept. In the winter, snow blew in through the windows and settled on the roof, melting and dripping down on his papers. The stove smoked so much that when he lit his morning fire, he could not see from one end of the room to the other. Not as patient as Clemens, the other officeholders began to drift away, until all that remained of the appointed government were the territorial secretary and the governor.

The territorial legislature met in October 1861, in a barnlike building with sawdust on the floor (which took the place of spittoons). The legislature divided the territory into nine counties, established county seats, and finally provided the most basic elements of law and order that had long been lacking.

By now, the nation was deeply involved in the Civil War. To care for the vast number of sick and wounded, the United States

Carson City in the late 1800s

government established the Sanitary Commission, a forerunner of the American Red Cross. Nevadans, though far removed from the scenes of battle, were anxious to contribute. What may have been the first national fund-raising campaign began in the mining town of Austin.

Among the small but outspoken group of southern sympathizers in Nevada was Austin grocer Reuel Gridley. When he lost an election bet, Gridley had to carry a 50-pound (23-kilogram) sack of flour decorated with Union flags down Austin's main street. With the Austin Brass Band playing and Union supporters cheering, the grocer donated his sack of flour to the Sanitary Fund. The sack was then auctioned for donations, each buyer giving it back so it could be auctioned again.

At the end of that day in April 1864, Gridley's "Sanitary Sack of Flour" had brought in more than $6,000. Gridley, who soon

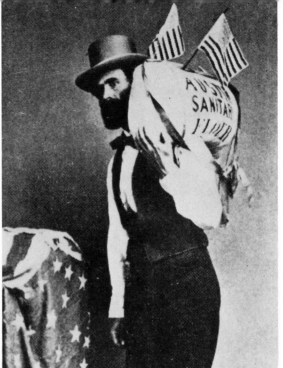

James Nye (left) served as Nevada's territorial governor. Reuel Gridley (right) raised money for the Union war effort with his famous "Sanitary Sack of Flour."

became a convert to the Union cause, took it to the Virginia City area, where generous bidding brought in another $40,000. The grocer spent a year traveling with his flour sack, selling it over and over for a grand total of $265,000—all for charity. Ironically, because of his absence, his business back in Austin went bankrupt.

The gold and silver from Nevada's mines were of vital importance to the nation, helping the Union to meet its huge wartime expenses. Though Nevada had only one-sixth of the population required for statehood, President Lincoln did everything in his power to help the territory become a state. An amendment to the Constitution abolishing slavery had just been approved by Congress, and the president needed to bring in one more loyal state to ratify it.

The way was paved for statehood, and all Nevada had to do was submit a constitution that was acceptable to its citizens. This took longer than expected, however. The state's mine owners objected to the first constitution because it included a provision taxing the mines. A second convention was then held, and this time the constitution was accepted. Because time was running short, the entire document was telegraphed to Washington, D.C., at the staggering cost of $3,416.77.

President Lincoln officially proclaimed Nevada a state on October 31, 1864, adding a thirty-sixth star to the nation's flag. Henry Goode Blasdel became the first elected governor of Nevada, and James Nye and William Stewart became the state's first United States senators. Nye and Stewart rushed to Washington to vote for the Thirteenth Amendment, abolishing slavery. Six months later, on April 9, 1865, the Civil War ended in a Union victory.

Five days after the Confederate forces surrendered, Abraham Lincoln was assassinated by a southern sympathizer. Nevadans deeply grieved the loss of this great president. The streets of Virginia City were thronged with citizens dressed in mourning. Every store, bank, and saloon was closed, the mills were shut down, and the church bells rang all day.

Though Nevada had achieved statehood, its boundaries were still not clearly established. The western boundary was settled after sheriffs' posses from Nevada and California clashed in the short-lived Sagebrush War.

The state's present eastern boundary remained some 50 miles (80 kilometers) inside Utah Territory until 1866, and the extreme southern triangle was part of Arizona Territory until 1867.

That a small outpost called Las Vegas might have remained in Arizona made little difference to the miners and politicians of early Nevada, who were not yet interested in regions so far removed from the Comstock Lode.

Chapter 6
FROM BOOM TO BUST

FROM BOOM TO BUST

LIFE ON THE COMSTOCK

Many of the miners who had flocked to the Comstock Lode soon sent for their families, and schools, churches, and other signs of a stable community began to take hold. Still, a certain element of wildness characterized life on the Comstock. The miners, facing constant danger underground, spent their earnings recklessly, giving little thought to the future.

The worst mine disaster in Nevada's history occurred in the spring of 1869, when a fire started in the Yellow Jacket mine at Gold Hill. Dozens of miners trapped in the network of tunnels could not be reached by rescuers because of the smoke and intense heat. Thirty-seven died, and in some sections of the mine, fires burned for years.

Between 1864 and 1881, the Comstock Lode produced hundreds of millions of dollars' worth of silver and gold. Virginia City grew into a rich mining community with first-class restaurants, an opera house, and fabulous mansions. Its six-story International Hotel boasted the first elevator west of Chicago.

Every traveling celebrity of the day was drawn to Virginia City, including two American presidents (Rutherford B. Hayes and Ulysses S. Grant), and inventor Thomas Edison. Famous actors and actresses put Virginia City's Piper's Opera House on their itineraries. Murals painted by some of the nation's best-known artists hung in the more elegant of Virginia City's more than a hundred saloons and gambling houses.

During the heyday of the Comstock Lode, some of the nation's most famous performers appeared at Piper's Opera House in fashionable Virginia City.

One of the earliest fortunes made on the Comstock produced the Bowers Mansion in Washoe Valley, now a museum. Eilley Orrum, perhaps the first white woman on the Comstock, had begun life as a poor girl in Scotland. She ran a boardinghouse in Gold Canyon, where she had a small claim at Gold Hill. Eilley married one of her boarders, Lemuel S. "Sandy" Bowers, who had a claim next to hers. In 1860, they struck it rich when gold and silver were discovered on their adjoining claims.

Unlearned and overly trusting, the Bowers set out on a spending spree in Europe. They lavished vast sums of money on furnishings for a mansion that was built during their absence. For a few years, they lived extravagantly, Sandy claiming that they had "money to throw to the birds." But when Sandy died, in 1868, Eilley found herself deeply in debt. She tried to hold onto her mansion by renting rooms and allowing the estate to be used for public functions. Eventually, she lost everything. For a

Eilley Bowers (above) and her husband Sandy built a mansion near Carson City (left) after striking it rich on the Comstock Lode.

while, she earned her living telling fortunes as the "Washoe Seeress." In 1903, Eilley died alone, as poor as she had started out.

Most of the surviving monuments of the Comstock's glory were built during Virginia City's greatest years—from 1875 to 1877. A fire destroyed a large part of the city on October 26, 1875. It roared through the streets with a terrible force, consuming churches, businesses, mills, and hundreds of homes in its path. A strong wind was blowing from the west, and efforts to contain the many blazes proved futile. Firefighters focused on keeping the flames from moving down the mine shafts. Much of the center of the city was destroyed, but rebuilding took place immediately. Virginia City had every intention of remaining the Queen of the West, though her glory days were numbered.

"CANARIES," CAMELS, COACHES, AND A RAILROAD

During those early days, transportation was a challenge for Nevadans. The miners had brought burros (donkeys) with them

Before railroads (left) arrived in the late 1860s, Nevadans tried several solutions to their transportation problems, including camels (right).

over the Sierra. Nicknamed the "Washoe canaries," these mischievous burros stole flour, sugar, bacon, beans, and anything else they could eat. They even devoured gunnysacks and old woolen shirts—but only after the miners left camp.

In 1861, thirteen camels imported from Mongolia were brought over the Sierra and put to work hauling salt (used for milling) from a dry salt marsh southeast of the Comstock. The camels thrived in the desert. But because they scared the horses and donkeys into running away, throwing riders, and overturning wagons, Virginia City passed an ordinance prohibiting them from entering the city during certain hours of the day. The use of camels for transportation was soon abandoned.

Freight wagons and stagecoaches were a common sight in Virginia City. By 1865, several stage companies were running full every day and charging high rates.

Mining had been largely responsible for the settlement of western and central Nevada. Railroad construction, however, caused the founding of several new towns in northern Nevada along the old Humboldt-Truckee pioneer route. The Central Pacific Railroad Company built part of the transcontinental rail line along this route in 1868 and 1869.

The Central Pacific had started construction in Sacramento, California, in 1863. When the tracks reached as far east as Truckee Meadows in Nevada, crews encountered some farms and an inn owned by Myron C. Lake, but no town. Lake told construction superintendent Charles Crocker that he would donate some of his land for a town site if Crocker would build a station and establish a distribution center there. The new town was named in honor of General Jesse L. Reno, a Union officer who had been killed in the Civil War. Within a few months, Reno was a bustling community.

In the brutal heat of summer, construction of the railroad continued across the Forty-Mile Desert and along the Humboldt. The multiracial work crews included thousands of Chinese. But the Chinese, who also had come to work the mines, were not made to feel welcome in Nevada. By 1890, most Chinese, pressured by anti-Chinese laws and other forms of racial discrimination, had left Nevada.

The small town of Winnemucca was already in existence when the Central Pacific entered in 1868. As railroad crews pushed swiftly eastward, such towns as Carlin and Elko sprang to life. The Central Pacific finally connected with the Union Pacific—whose crews were laying track from the east—at Promontory, Utah. On May 10, 1869, a golden spike from California and a silver spike from Nevada were driven into place, completing the first railroad to cross the continent from coast to coast.

In 1870, Nevada gained widespread attention when it became the site of the first train robbery in the West. Masked men stopped a train near Verdi, a station about 10 miles (16 kilometers) west of

Reno, and took a Wells Fargo strongbox containing $40,000 in gold coins. The shocking news was flashed throughout the United States and Europe.

Until it was bought by the Southern Pacific in 1899, the Central Pacific was Nevada's most important railroad. However, many smaller lines also served the state. The Virginia & Truckee, the richest and most famous short line of the 1800s, brought silver ore from the Comstock down to Carson City. The V & T wrapped around the rugged landscape in amazing curves, trestles, and tunnels and was called the "crookedest railroad in the world."

Connected by rail to the rest of the country, its mines bustling and its towns growing, Nevada was, by 1870, important enough to be given a branch of the United States Mint. Opening at Carson City in January, the mint eliminated the need to send the refined metals to the mint in San Francisco. Between 1870 and the closing of the operation in 1893, nearly $50 million worth of coins were produced in Carson City.

THE BANK CROWD AND THE BONANZA KINGS

One of the least popular men on the Comstock was William P. Sharon, who managed the Bank of California at Virginia City. Sharon and the "California Bank Crowd" gained control of some of the most important mills and mines and made huge fortunes for themselves. But their dominance of the lode did not go unchallenged.

John Mackay, an Irishman who had started out as a mine timberman, managed to acquire a small fortune on the Comstock. He formed a partnership with three other Irishmen—James G. Fair, James C. Flood, and William O'Brian—and the four men gained control of a section of the lode.

An early photograph of the U.S. Mint in Carson City

In the spring of 1873, Mackay's men discovered one of the richest—perhaps *the* richest—bodies of gold and silver ore ever found on earth. The "Big Bonanza" was nearly a quarter mile (0.4 kilometer) beneath the surface, directly under Virginia City. It would produce over $100 million worth of ore and make Mackay and the other three "Bonanza Kings" the powerful new leaders on the Comstock.

Another challenge to the Bank Crowd came from Adolph Sutro, a German immigrant and engineer. In 1869, he began construction of a great tunnel that would extend some 4 miles (6 kilometers) into the lower depths of the lode. Sutro's Tunnel would make it easier to mine the ore and to drain the often steaming-hot water that flooded the mines. But the Bank Crowd feared the tunnel would make Sutro the most powerful man on the Comstock. They did everything they could to delay the tremendous engineering project.

By the time the massive engineering project known as Sutro's Tunnel was finished, the Comstock Lode was nearly depleted.

Sutro's Tunnel was finally completed in 1878. It could have saved the mining companies millions of dollars in pumping expenses and prevented tragedies like the deaths in the Yellow Jacket fire. But it came too late. By 1878, most of the rich ore of the Comstock Lode was gone. The era of fabulous riches had come to an end.

TWENTY YEARS OF DEPRESSION

Exploring the abandoned mines on the Comstock in the 1890s, author Dan DeQuille described the ghostly sight:

> Down in these deserted and dreary old levels, hundreds of feet beneath the surface . . . [are] fungi of monstrous growth, and most uncouth and uncanny form. They cover the old posts in great moist, dew-distilling masses and descend from the timbers overhead in broad slimy curtains or hang down like long squirming serpents. . . .

Beyond the light of his flickering candle flame, he could hear no sound but the steady drip of water.

The decline of the Comstock Lode was paralleled by the passing of other Nevada mining booms, such as those at Austin, Eureka, and Pioche. Between 1880 and 1900, Nevada's population declined from sixty-two thousand to a mere forty-two thousand. Carson City was a tiny state capital, Lake Tahoe had a few resorts, and a scant amount of trade was carried on among a few towns.

With mining in a slump, agriculture became the stable industry of the state. Farming and ranching had been going on before the advent of mining, but had taken second place to the more exciting pursuit of silver and gold.

In the 1850s, N. H. A. Mason drove a band of cattle from California into the Walker River region, which later came to be known as Mason Valley. This was the beginning of a vast cattle and ranching empire. Fred Dangberg, a native of Germany, began another large ranching enterprise in the 1850s. Dangberg settled in Carson Valley, a few miles from Genoa, and eventually became the owner of more than 35,000 acres (14,164 hectares) of land. Others prospered in Smith Valley, a rich agricultural area much like Carson Valley.

One of the earliest sheepherders in Nevada was Pedro Altube, a Basque from the Pyrenees Mountains between Spain and France. In 1859, seeing a similarity between Nevada's mountains and his native Pyrenees, Altube established the Spanish Ranch in the Elko region. Basques were to become a picturesque part of northern Nevada's landscape.

The livestock industry, which had grown during the mining booms, continued to expand in the 1880s. Ranching took hold along the Humboldt River at such places as Big Meadows (now Lovelock). Elko became a major cattle center and railroad town.

Ranchers shipped their cattle and sheep by rail to more populated areas and opened up new markets. In the 1890s, however, the industry was hit by a depression that many cattlemen and sheepmen did not survive. Some of those who did, including Jewett W. Adams (who became a governor of Nevada) and William N. McGill, managed to build great ranching empires.

Another rancher to become a governor of the state was John Sparks, who introduced Hereford cattle to Nevada. Herefords became the most common type of range animal in the state. The community of Sparks, near Reno, was named after the governor.

In the last part of the nineteenth century, too many cattle and sheep were driven onto the Nevada ranges, and overgrazing became a serious problem. There was not enough water and grass for both cattle and sheep. Congress attempted to solve the problem in 1934 with the passage of the Taylor Grazing Act, which divided the open range between the cattlemen and sheepmen and required the ranchers to pay grazing fees.

Two important issues dominated Nevada politics between 1880 and 1900: the need for irrigation and the silver controversy. Congress had decided to stop making nearly all silver coins, causing the price of silver to drop. In 1892, Nevadans formed the Silver party to fight this action on the national level. In 1896, the state's Democrats adopted a "Free Silver" plank and took over the Silver party; thereafter, they were known as the Silver-Democrats.

Another kind of fight in Nevada drew national attention—a boxing match that was the state's first attempt to attract tourist dollars. In 1897, when boxing was not considered a respectable sport in the United States, Nevada lawmakers passed a bill to license prizefights. The first spectacular fight, between James J. "Gentleman Jim" Corbett and Robert Fitzsimmons, ended in the fourteenth round, with the underdog Fitzsimmons knocking

The boxing match between "Gentleman Jim" Corbett and Bob Fitzsimmons, held in Carson City in 1897, was the first fight ever filmed.

out Corbett. The fight's promoters took advantage of something new called "moving pictures," and a film made of the fight grossed three-quarters of a million dollars. This film was the first ever made of a fight. Since then, Nevada has played host to some of the most exciting world-championship boxing matches ever held.

During Nevada's *borrasca* period (the opposite of bonanza), prospectors continued to roam the hills and deserts in search of new finds. From time to time, they turned up small deposits of precious metals, but nothing to match the Comstock.

A small gold rush in the 1890s led to the founding of Delamar, near Pioche, in southeastern Nevada. Delamar produced $15 million worth of ore. But by 1900, it was on its way to becoming another of Nevada's ghost towns.

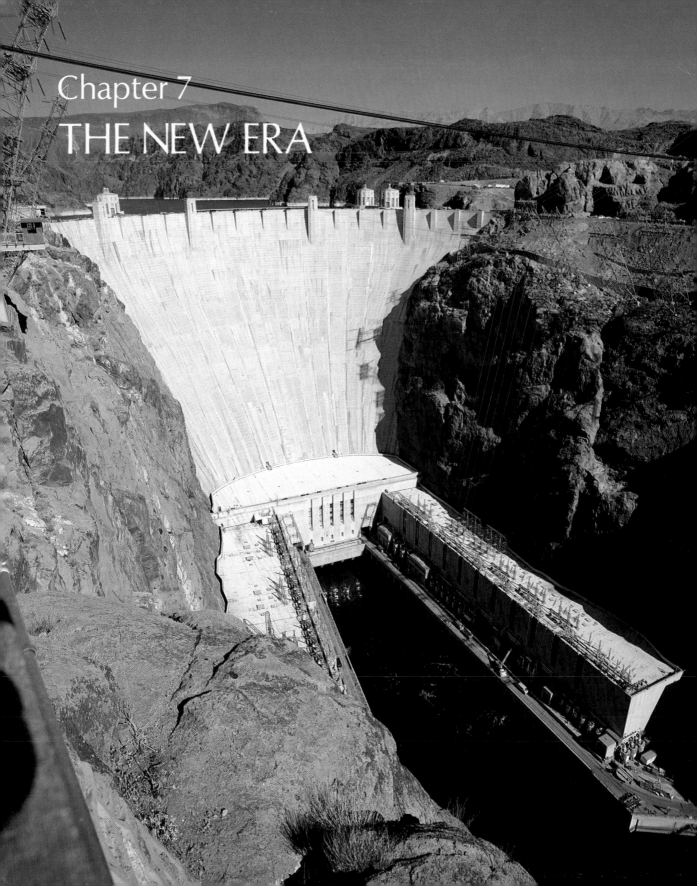

Chapter 7
THE NEW ERA

THE NEW ERA

In 1899, only the most optimistic prospectors dreamed of another gold or silver mining boom. But no one could have imagined the value that Nevada's nonprecious minerals, still buried beneath the ground, would have in the twentieth century.

In a state where water was scarce—except in the mines, where it wasn't wanted—irrigation would transform the desert. Moreover, a new machine, the automobile, was about to revolutionize transportation.

THE TONOPAH-GOLDFIELD BOOM

In the spring of 1900, a rancher and part-time prospector named James Butler camped one night by a spring that the Indians called Tonopah. The next morning, he looked for one of his burros, which had strayed away. He found the burro under a rock ledge that looked so rich, Butler broke off a piece, intending to have it assayed (analyzed). He took it to Tasker L. Oddie, then district attorney of Nye County. Butler promised Oddie a share in the mine if he could get the sample assayed. What became known as the Mizpah vein proved to be so rich in silver that a new town sprang up around it almost overnight.

Within a few years, Tonopah was a sprawling city of three thousand people, and by 1905, it was the county seat. Automobiles had become so numerous that the town had to establish what was probably Nevada's first speed limit: 4 miles (6.4 kilometers) per hour.

59

United States Army troops were sent in when miners in Goldfield went on strike in 1907.

The last great gold rush of the West gave birth to the town of Goldfield, 30 miles (48 kilometers) south of Tonopah. By 1905, more than six thousand people from all over the world were living in Goldfield. But most of the mines were controlled by two mine owners: George Wingfield and his partner George S. Nixon.

George Nixon was already famous as the banker from Winnemucca who had been held up by Butch Cassidy and his gang. It is true that on September 19, 1900, Nixon was held up with a knife at his throat. However, contrary to myth, the infamous Cassidy was not on the scene.

From Goldfield, Nixon went on to become a United States senator, leaving Wingfield to run the mines. Wingfield faced a challenge in 1907 when the miners in Goldfield went on strike. A radical group called the Industrial Workers of the World (IWW) had gained control over the more compliant miners' unions.

Across the country, IWW members were agitating for better working conditions and calling for the overthrow of capitalism.

To preserve the status quo, Wingfield persuaded Governor John Sparks to wire President Theodore Roosevelt to send army units to Goldfield. This labor dispute—the most serious in the state's history—led to the founding of the Nevada State Police.

Goldfield reached a population of about twenty thousand at its peak. On picture postcards, tiny Las Vegas boasted that it was the "gateway to Goldfield." But after 1910, production at Goldfield declined, and the town with it.

At the time that gold and silver production in Nevada declined, American industry began to need increasing amounts of copper. Copper ore had been discovered in the Ely area of White Pine County, as well as in many other places in Nevada. By 1911, the mines near Ely were producing more profitably than those in Goldfield or Tonopah. Copper became the state's most important mineral resource and would remain so for fifty years.

POLITICS IN THE PROGRESSIVE ERA

The Progressive Era, the period between 1900 and 1917, saw a popular revolt against control of government and business by a privileged few. Reformers across the country were demanding greater democracy in every aspect of American life.

In Nevada, the Tonopah-Goldfield rush brought a complete change in the political scene. The leaders of the twentieth-century boomtowns did not have the connections with California banking and railroad interests that had corrupted Comstock politics. Tonopah men like Tasker Oddie, who became governor of Nevada and later a United States senator, took over the state's affairs.

The most important national political figure to come out of Tonopah during this time was Key Pittman. Born in Mississippi, Pittman had participated in the Klondike rush in Alaska, and joined those who stormed to Tonopah at news of the strike. He had studied some law, and established a law office in Tonopah. Pittman was a colorful character, known for his gracious southern manner, fondness for strong drink, and habit of carrying a pistol.

In 1912, after George Nixon's death, Nevadans chose Key Pittman to replace the popular senator. In the nation's capital, Pittman was able to help Nevada's mining industry. In 1918, Congress passed the Pittman Act, by which the federal government promised to buy a certain amount of silver each year until 1923.

During the Great Depression of the 1930s, President Franklin D. Roosevelt appointed Senator Pittman to be one of the United States representatives at the World Economic Conference in London. In the years just before World War II, Senator Pittman served as chairman of the powerful Foreign Relations Committee.

Nevada's senior senator during the early 1900s was Francis G. Newlands, a man in tune with the times. He was the driving force behind the Reclamation Act of 1902 (known as the Newlands Act), a major Progressive measure that empowered the government to build dams and irrigation projects in the West. Under this act, the Newlands Irrigation Project opened 87,000 acres (35,208 hectares) of west-central Nevada desert for irrigation, launching a new phase of economic growth in the state.

During the first decades of the twentieth century, Nevada followed the lead of other Progressive states by passing much-needed labor legislation. The new legislation ensured an eight-hour workday, industrial safety laws, industrial accident insurance, and special laws for working women. A number of commissions were created to regulate banking, railroads, and telegraph and telephone companies. The state also made reforms in education and health. A compulsory attendance law was

In the early 1900s, Senator Francis Newlands sponsored federal legislation that made possible the irrigation of thousands of acres of Nevada desert.

passed, vocational education and standard textbooks were introduced, new schools and libraries were built, and pure food and drug laws were passed. In 1909, Nevada's most avid reformers succeeded in outlawing all gambling in the state. Illegal gambling continued to thrive in most communities, however, and in 1931, a momentous reversal would take place.

WORLD WAR I AND THE 1920s

When World War I broke out in Europe in August 1914, George Wingfield, the economic "boss" of Nevada, predicted that it would give the state "a gilt-edged market for all her products." Wingfield foresaw a big demand for Nevada's sheep and beef, a strong market for its horses, and a greater need for the state's minerals. Happily for Nevada, his prediction proved to be correct.

Reno, which attracted large numbers of tourists after gambling was legalized in the 1930s (right), has also long been a popular place to get married (left).

The United States did not enter the war until the spring of 1917. In addition to those Nevadans who were drafted, Nevada sent 1,447 volunteers into the regular army, making Nevada a state with one of the highest rates of participation in proportion to its population. Nevada's sons were sent to war with large patriotic demonstrations.

The war effort prevented the nation from building roads for its growing number of automobiles. After the war ended in 1918, however, a transcontinental network of highways shot across the nation, with the federal government matching state funds to pay for it. In the 1920s, Nevada celebrated the completion of two east-west highways across the state: the Victory Highway (today's Interstate 80) along the old Humboldt route; and the Lincoln Highway (today's U.S. Highway 50), farther south.

In the 1920s, Reno became known as the "divorce capital of the world." Since the early part of the century, Nevada had attracted

Patrons at a Reno casino in 1931, the year gambling was legalized in Nevada

temporary residents who were seeking a faster divorce than other states offered. In 1927, Nevada passed a law allowing a person to obtain a divorce after living in the state for only three months. It was easier to get married in Nevada, as well, and in the years to come, automobiles on the new highways would bring increasing numbers of visitors anxious to alter their marital status. In 1931, the residency period required to obtain a divorce was reduced even further—to a mere six weeks. Gambling was legalized the same year, provoking out-of-staters to say, "If you can't do it at home, go to Nevada."

DEPRESSION AND WAR

In the 1930s, the world plunged into the worst depression in history. By 1932, more than 13 million Americans were unemployed—a staggering 25 percent of the labor force. The number of jobless and homeless grew day by day, and those who had saved their money were not spared—5,504 American banks failed between 1930 and 1933.

Nevada, not being an industrial state, was not hit quite as hard as many other states. But the collapse of George Wingfield's chain of twelve banks was a blow to the state's ailing livestock industry. Wingfield had been supportive of the stockmen, and with his support gone, many were forced into bankruptcy. Nevada farmers lost much of their land to Pacific Coast and eastern interests. Simultaneously, mineral production in the state reached its lowest point.

Under President Franklin D. Roosevelt's New Deal, a number of federal projects were set in motion to restore the country's economic health. Nevadans particularly benefited from these programs. The Civilian Conservation Corps (CCC) employed nearly four thousand Nevadans between 1933 and 1939 to build roads, dig canals and irrigation ditches, plant trees, and aid conservation. The Works Progress Administration (WPA) put Nevadans to work on many community projects, including the building of schools, public buildings, and swimming pools.

The construction of Boulder (now Hoover) Dam required thousands of workmen using some of the largest equipment in the world. Working in temperatures of up to 130 degrees Fahrenheit (54 degrees Celsius), laborers poured nearly 7 million tons (6.4 million metric tons) of concrete into a steep canyon on the Colorado River. Boulder City was created to house the workers. The dam was completed in 1936; its name was changed to Hoover Dam in 1947. The increased trade and traffic generated by the presence of the dam resulted in the boom of a once-sleepy village that lay only 25 miles (40 kilometers) away—Las Vegas.

The outbreak of World War II shook the entire nation out of its economic slump and brought increased federal involvement in

Hoover Dam, constructed in the 1930s (left), stores irrigation water and provides hydroelectric power (right) for a large part of the Southwest.

Nevada. A United States Navy ammunition depot had been completed near Hawthorne in 1930. A decade later, the possibility that the West Coast might be attacked resulted in the establishment of military bases in Nevada near Fallon, Reno, Tonopah, and Las Vegas.

The war also elicited heavy demands for copper and other minerals, further stimulating Nevada's economy. But gambling and tourism combined were already surpassing mining and agriculture as the state's most important industry.

Legalized gambling and easy liquor sales made Nevada towns attractive to the large number of servicemen in both Nevada and California. The many people who came to the Pacific Coast to work in its defense plants were also drawn to Nevada's entertainment. Billboards appeared along highways across the nation, luring visitors to a well-known Reno casino with the slogan HAROLDS CLUB OR BUST! Harolds Club began counting its daily visitors by the ten thousands.

Patrick McCarran (second from left), shown here with constituents, was a powerful member of Congress in the mid-1900s.

With the end of the war in 1945, restrictions on travel were removed and tourists flocked to Nevada. In 1946, the fabulous Flamingo Hotel—the first hotel-casino—opened in Las Vegas, and there was no stopping the city's growth toward becoming the "Entertainment Capital of the World." The Flamingo was built by Benjamin "Bugsy" Siegel, a New Yorker who was a "front man" for organized crime. His shady dealings resulted in his murder in 1947. Many of the other hotel-casinos that followed also were run by gangsters or had underworld connections. Organized crime was able to infiltrate Las Vegas gambling in the 1940s because until 1954, banks and other conventional financial sources would not finance casinos.

One of the greatest problems the Nevada government had to face after the war was the supervision of gambling. Congress came close to passing a bill that would have taxed every casino in Nevada out of business. But Patrick A. McCarran, one of Nevada's most colorful and powerful senators, labored to save the gambling industry—in spite of his objection to the state's growing dependency on its revenues.

By the end of the 1940s, Senator McCarran, whose political career had begun in Tonopah, had won control of Nevada politics.

The legendary senator had a reputation as a maverick and a plain-spoken individualist. He was directly involved in the creation of what would become the Federal Aviation Administration. Because of his work in airport development, the large airport that opened in Las Vegas in 1947 was named after him.

In later years, Senator McCarran became chairman of the Judiciary Committee and a ranking member of the Appropriations Committee. He sponsored the Internal Security Act, aimed at controlling the alleged Communist threat; and the McCarran-Walter Act, which tightened controls on immigrants and aliens. Though a powerful member of Congress, he never forgot his constituents. He is said to have called a rancher in northeastern Nevada one day and asked him for a favor. "There's a miner up Tuscarora Canyon who broke his chopping arm and can't get in his winter wood," said the senator. "Would you take a couple of truckloads up for him?"

MODERN NEVADA

Since 1950, the flood of people into the western states has added to Nevada's population, as well as to its tourist and gaming industry. This has caused a demand for more schools, housing, and government services.

In the 1950s, Governor Charles Russell brought needed reforms to the state in a number of areas, including the gambling industry. In 1955, in an effort to keep gangsters out of Nevada gambling, Governor Russell created a gaming control board that investigated the backgrounds of applicants for the license required to operate a casino. The governors who followed Russell expanded upon the elaborate system that was created to keep gambling operations in check. But in 1961, United States Attorney General Robert

Kennedy launched an attack against Nevada gambling. Some of the state's casinos had been "skimming": taking money "off the top" of their taxable income and not paying taxes on it. Kennedy's "war on Nevada" resulted in federal convictions.

In the 1960s, prominent businessmen began to acquire interests in Nevada's casinos. This was encouraged by the passage, in 1967, of a state law allowing corporate ownership of casinos. The new law was a further attempt by the state legislature to keep organized crime out of the gaming industry. Eccentric billionaire Howard Hughes, a famous moviemaker and wartime aircraft producer, purchased several casinos and other properties in the Las Vegas area. Hughes and other corporate investors gave gaming a more respectable appearance, and today, corporate ownership of casinos is a major force in Nevada's gambling industry.

By the 1970s, with Nevada's population concentrated in the metropolitan areas of Las Vegas and Reno, air and water pollution were becoming a serious problem. During the administration of Governor Paul Laxalt, Nevada joined with California to fight pollution of Lake Tahoe. In 1986, the Tahoe Regional Planning Agency adopted a new master plan that would strictly regulate growth in the area through the year 2006.

The greater part of Nevada remains rural, partly because the land is federally owned. In the "Sagebrush Rebellion" of the early 1980s, Nevada tried to gain state control of some 50 million acres (20 million hectares). But over 85 percent of the state continues to be administered by the federal government. Most of this land is controlled by the Bureau of Land Management (BLM), an agency of the Department of the Interior. The rest is divided among the army, navy, air force, and Department of Energy.

In December 1950, the United States Atomic Energy Commission (AEC) designated a section of the Las Vegas Bombing

In 1951, the United States government began testing atomic bombs at the Nevada Test Site.

and Gunnery Range for the testing of atomic bombs. With the first explosion at the Nevada Test Site on January 27, 1951, the state became a natural laboratory for some of the most ominous scientific experiments in the history of mankind. Since the signing of the Nuclear Test Ban Treaty in 1963, which prohibited atmospheric explosions, all the nuclear testing at the site has been conducted underground.

Today, the Nevada Test Site is one of the major employers of southern Nevada. Even so, it is a continuing source of controversy. The possible effects of downwind radiation from the site concern many Nevada residents, and the test site draws thousands of antinuclear protestors every year from all over the country. Another controversial federal project being considered for the state is the hotly debated Nuclear Waste Repository.

Nevada presents a striking contrast between the old western frontier and the frontiers of modern technology. Military jets practice maneuvers high above the ranges where wild horses and burros still roam.

Chapter 8
GOVERNMENT AND THE ECONOMY

GOVERNMENT AND THE ECONOMY

The people of Nevada enjoy one of the lightest tax burdens in the nation. As one of the fastest-growing states, Nevada is proud of its ability to meet increasing government costs while keeping taxes low.

Nevada is one of seven states without a personal income tax and one of only five that does not tax business corporations. It is the only state that does not have an inheritance tax. However, Nevada collects more amusement taxes than any other state. Millions of dollars in sales taxes are the largest source of the state's revenues, followed by gambling taxes.

STATE GOVERNMENT

Nevada is governed under its original constitution, adopted in 1864. But the constitution has since been amended to meet the state's changing needs.

Nevada's government, like that of most other states, is patterned after the federal government. It is divided into three branches: the legislative branch, which makes laws; the executive branch, which enforces laws; and the judicial branch, which interprets laws.

The executive branch is headed by the governor and the lieutenant governor, who are elected to four-year terms. Key state officials, including the secretary of state, treasurer, controller, and attorney general, are also elected to four-year terms.

Nevada's legislature consists of a twenty-one-member senate and a forty-two-member assembly. Members of the senate serve four-year terms; members of the assembly serve two-year terms. Nevada's legislature meets every odd-numbered year in January, in sessions that last four to six months. Most of the work of the legislature is done not in these formal meetings of the full house, but in committees. The senate has nine committees, and the assembly, thirteen. Each committee deals with a broad area such as education, health and welfare, or commerce. There are also interim committees that work while the legislature is not in session.

Nevada's judicial branch is headed by a supreme court, to which five justices are elected for six-year terms. The state has nine district courts. At the local level are justice courts, small claims courts, and municipal courts, which handle misdemeanors.

Locally, Nevada is divided into sixteen counties plus Carson City, which is a consolidated city-county. The county is the primary unit of local government. Each county has a board of commissioners and other elected officials. Each of Nevada's eighteen incorporated cities has a government board, usually called a city council, headed by a mayor.

Because Nevada is still so small in population, Nevadans can personally go to almost anyone in state government—even the governor—not just to express concerns, but to get responses.

EDUCATION

The first plans for a tax-supported school system were made while Nevada was still a territory. In 1865, a year after statehood, the legislature created the first school districts. In some sparsely populated areas, schools were attended by as few as three or four children, who sat on boxes in rickety little buildings. Until 1900, the state had only a few high schools.

Nevada's government buildings range from Virginia City's classic Storey County Courthouse (left) to Las Vegas's strikingly modern City Hall (above).

Today, Nevada has 17 school districts, one for each county and Carson City. There are 53 high schools, 27 junior highs, 15 middle schools, 194 elementary schools, and 10 special schools, for a combined state total of 299. All children in the state between the ages of seven and seventeen are required by law to attend school.

The University of Nevada system began with one campus in Elko in 1874. Twelve years later, the campus was moved to Reno. A southern branch, now the University of Nevada-Las Vegas, was established in the 1950s. In 1988, the university opened an International Division in Tokyo, Japan, offering English language instruction for Japanese students.

The Desert Research Institute in Reno is a small part of the university system. The Mackay School of Mines, located on the Reno campus, is one of the world's leading mining schools. It was endowed by Clarence Mackay, the son of "Bonanza King" John Mackay. Nevada also has an extensive two-year community college system with four main campuses. Sierra Nevada College, in Incline Village, is a private liberal arts school.

Tourism is Nevada's leading industry.

TOURISM

Tourism is by far Nevada's most important industry. Every year, some 30 million people visit Nevada, attracted by the bright lights, big games, first-class hotels, and exciting nightlife of the entertainment industry. A wide variety of outdoor activities, sporting events, and special cultural performances add to the state's unique appeal.

Tourists spend billions of dollars a year in Nevada, a large percentage of it at the gaming tables and slot machines. Gaming has made Nevada's border towns its most recent boomtowns. In the 1980s, Wendover, Jackpot, Laughlin, and Mesquite mushroomed into gambling meccas, attracting visitors from bordering states where gambling remains illegal.

Gaming and tourism account for as much as 80 percent of Nevada's gross state product (the total value of all goods and services produced in the state each year). Recently, the state has been making strong efforts to diversify its economy so that

Placer mining (above) is one of the methods used to extract Nevada's vast mineral deposits, which include gold (top left), and silver and turquoise (left).

Nevadans will not be totally dependent upon one industry. This may ultimately benefit Nevada in other ways, because casino gambling is related to a number of social problems, including high crime, suicide, and high alcohol and drug use.

NATURAL RESOURCES

Nevada's vast mineral deposits are among its most important natural resources. Nevada is the nation's leading producer of gold, magnesite (used in steel manufacturing), and mercury. By the late 1980s, the state was well into its second gold rush, producing more than half the gold mined in the United States. In fact, five of the nation's last seven gold discoveries have been in Nevada. Most of Nevada's working gold mines lie in the central part of the state.

Nevada is a leading producer of silver, and the world's largest producer of turquoise. In 1954, a turquoise nugget weighing 152 pounds (69 kilograms) was found in Lander County near Battle Mountain. The world's largest black opal, now displayed in the

Nevada's beautiful scenery is one of its most valuable natural resources.

Smithsonian Institution in Washington, D.C., was found in Humboldt County in 1927.

Most of Nevada's mineral production comes from the northern two-thirds of the state. The extreme southern region produces gypsum, limestone, and clays. Petroleum has been found in some central areas of Nevada, and oil, gas, and geothermal resources are just beginning to be developed.

Nevada's wide-open spaces and beautiful scenery are the state's other natural resources.

FARMING AND RANCHING

Ranching is Nevada's most important agricultural activity; more than 85 percent of the state's farm and ranch land is devoted to raising livestock. The average size of Nevada's 2,400 farms and ranches is 3,667 acres (1,484 hectares). The largest ranches, however, cover as much as 275,000 acres (111,290 hectares).

A Nevada sheepherder tending his flock

Water is the state's most limited resource, and in drought years, like 1988, farmers and ranchers have had to fight for their lives. "If you've got land without water, you've got dirt," says Dave Fulstone, a Yerington farmer and member of the Nevada Farm Bureau. "If you've got land and water, you've got a farm."

Most of the large cattle and sheep ranches in Nevada are in the northern counties, where Elko, Winnemucca, and Lovelock are the chief trading centers. Riding horses are also raised in many parts of the state.

Nevada's leading crop is alfalfa hay, which is used as winter feed for livestock. Barley, oats, wheat, and such vegetables as potatoes and onions are also grown in the state. These are produced in the western valleys near Fallon, Gardnerville, and

Livestock raising, Nevada's leading agricultural activity, is concentrated in the northern part of the state.

Yerington, as well as in some irrigated valleys in the north. Dairying is carried on in both the west and the south, and some of the southern valleys produce fruits, vegetables, and cotton.

MANUFACTURING AND TRADE

Five percent of Nevada's gross state product comes from manufacturing. More than eight hundred manufacturers produce a wide variety of products in Nevada. Based on the number of jobs, Reno is the leading manufacturing area in the state, with increasing production of electronics and other high-technology items.

In the Las Vegas area, much of the manufacturing occurs at the Henderson Industrial Complex, which has water and power available from nearby Hoover Dam. In the late 1980s, manufacturing firms began moving into North Las Vegas.

The Nevada Power Company plant in Las Vegas

Printing and publishing have become Nevada's largest manufacturing segment. A boom in the construction industry in the late 1980s reflected the state's growth and helped the income of Nevadans to be among the fastest rising in the nation.

THE FEDERAL GOVERNMENT

The federal government plays an important part in Nevada's economy. Federal involvement in the state began with the construction of Boulder (now Hoover) Dam in the 1930s. A United States Army Air Corps gunnery school established in southern Nevada during World War II later became Nellis Air Force Base. One of the nation's largest air force bases, Nellis covers more than 11,000 acres (4,452 hectares) of land northeast of

Las Vegas. It is a major contributor to Las Vegas's economy, providing some twenty-five thousand civilian jobs. The Nellis Range, used for supersonic and low-altitude combat training, covers more than 3 million acres (1.2 million hectares). Thousands of military personnel are stationed at Nellis and at the Fallon Naval Air Station, an important factor in the economy of the Fallon area. In the same way, the Hawthorne Army Depot is an essential part of Hawthorne's economy.

The Nevada Test Site (NTS) at Mercury is the world's largest government-run outdoor laboratory. Operated by the United States Department of Energy, the site covers approximately 1,350 square miles (3,497 square kilometers) of desert 50 miles (80 kilometers) north of Las Vegas. It is a major center for the development of nuclear weapons and peaceful uses of nuclear energy.

TRANSPORTATION

Nevada's vast size makes it heavily dependent on air transportation. The state has about sixty public and sixty private airports. Ranchers and farmers own most of the private airports. Nevada's major airports are Reno-Cannon International and McCarran International, both in Las Vegas. In the late 1980s, McCarran underwent a multimillion-dollar expansion to handle increasing numbers of tourists. It is one of the most modern airports in the world.

Union Pacific Railroad Company and Southern Pacific Transportation Company are the largest freight railroads servicing Nevada. Amtrak is a major passenger service through the state.

Nevada has about 50,000 miles (80,465 kilometers) of roads and highways, about a third of which are surfaced. Two of the nine federal highways are part of the interstate system. Several national bus lines and trucking lines serve the state.

In the 1990s, Las Vegas will become the showcase for a futuristic transportation system called a *people mover*. Construction of the MagLev system (short for Magnetic Levitation) began in 1988. The first of its kind in the United States, the Las Vegas People Mover will whisk passengers from one point to another in cars on elevated guide rails. The cars will be moved along, by electric current, on permanent magnets rather than on steel or rubber-tired wheels, eliminating noise and air pollution. Las Vegas is already considering a second MagLev system.

Because of the state's strategic location, warehousing and trucking industries flourish in Nevada. Much of the supplies and equipment shipped east and west across the United States must go through or over the state. Nevada's free port law encourages companies to store and process goods in the state by allowing tax exemptions for goods that are merely in transit.

COMMUNICATION

Nevada has more than fifty newspapers and other periodicals. Daily newspapers with the largest circulations include the *Las Vegas Review-Journal* and the *Reno Gazette-Journal*.

Nevada has twenty-eight AM and thirty-six FM radio stations, and ten television stations. The state's first radio station, KOH, began broadcasting from Reno in 1928. Nevada's first television stations, KOLO-TV in Reno and KLAS-TV in Las Vegas, were established in 1953.

The Churchill County Telephone & Telegraph System, formed in 1889, is the only county-owned and maintained telephone company in the United States.

Chapter 9
ARTS AND LEISURE

ARTS AND LEISURE

LITERARY NEVADA

Nevada's literary history began in the colorful mining towns that sprouted up in the 1800s. All of them had newspapers that rose and fell with the booming and busting of the mines. Some of the papers never grew beyond having tents for offices. An exception was Nevada's very first newspaper. The *Territorial Enterprise,* which began in Genoa in 1858 and was moved to Virginia City a few years later, became the most influential paper in the West and remained so for two decades.

One of the reporters for the *Enterprise,* William Wright (who wrote under the pen name Dan DeQuille), gave vivid descriptions of life on the Comstock. His book *The Big Bonanza* (originally published in 1876 as *History of the Big Bonanza*) is an accurate and animated history of the fabulous Comstock Lode.

Another reporter, Samuel Langhorne Clemens, took the pen name Mark Twain while writing for the *Enterprise,* and quickly became known for his humorous blend of fact and fiction. The author of *The Adventures of Tom Sawyer* and *Huckleberry Finn,* Twain also wrote *Roughing It,* a tongue-in-cheek account of his adventures in Nevada.

In the 1880s, Sarah Winnemucca, the granddaughter of Paiute Chief Truckee, published *Life Among the Paiutes: Their Wrongs and Claims,* a fascinating account of Indian society in northwestern Nevada.

Left: The Reno Philharmonic during a
concert at Mormon Station State Park
Above: An actor portraying Mark Twain
at Piper's Opera House in Virginia City

The works of three other Nevada writers have gained national
attention. Walter Van Tilburg Clark's *Ox-Bow Incident* has been
called one of the best western novels ever written and was made
into a motion picture. Robert Laxalt won praise for *Sweet Promised
Land*, a tribute to his Basque immigrant father. Sessions Wheeler,
in his popular historical novel *Paiute*, dealt with the Pyramid Lake
War and the discovery of the Comstock Lode.

FINE ARTS AND CRAFTS

Nevada has come a long way since the 1870s, when Piper's
Opera House in Virginia City hosted Italian operas, vaudeville
shows, dog fights, and everything in between. In 1967, the Nevada
legislature established the Nevada State Council on the Arts to
boost cultural activities throughout the state. Two decades later,
the council's executive director reported with pride, "People are
stunned that a town the size of Reno has a regionally imported
opera company, an excellent symphony, a chamber orchestra, and

The cultures of Nevada's Native American groups are celebrated at festivals that feature food, dancing (right), and such traditional crafts as this Paiute cradleboard (far right).

a ballet company. And Las Vegas has the same thing." In fact, over a hundred organizations promote the arts in more than twenty Nevada towns and cities.

Las Vegas and Reno are frequent stops for classical as well as popular performances of world renown. Rural Nevadans, however, are not to be left out. They have been known to stroll, mud-spattered, from a pig-wrestling contest to a piano recital in an old railroad depot. Small towns may hold performances in the local saloon. In Yerington, the performing-arts center is a converted car garage called "the Autotorium." Many excellent little theater groups are active in Nevada. In addition to performances at the campuses of the university, stage performances are also given around the state in such towns as Elko and Fallon.

Preserving folk arts and crafts is important to Nevadans, from favorite family stories and recipes to dances, songs, and special skills. Numerous organizations promote a variety of handicrafts throughout the state. Traditional Indian arts and crafts, such as Paiute cradleboard making, have been revived on reservations.

Among Nevada's many interesting museums are the Las Vegas Museum of Natural History (left) and the Liberace Museum (above), also in Las Vegas.

The intricately designed baskets of nineteenth-century Washo basket maker Dat-So-La-Lee are prized museum pieces.

Nevada has about fifty local museums and more than forty libraries. The Nevada State Museum, located in the old federal mint building in Carson City, has a replica of a mine shaft and many relics of the Comstock. The Las Vegas Museum of Natural History features life-sized, computerized dinosaurs that roll their eyes as they move and roar. The Liberace Museum, also in Las Vegas, displays rare and antique pianos and the late entertainer's glittering costumes. Nevada's colorful history is the focus of the museum and research library at the Nevada Historical Society in Reno. Other interesting museums include the Nevada State Railroad Museum in Carson City and the Churchill County Museum in Fallon.

In both Las Vegas and Reno, the works of local and regional artists are shown year round in numerous galleries. Photography is a popular pursuit in Nevada as well; Nevada has the largest percentage of photographers of any state.

The Nevada State Museum in Carson City, housed in the former U.S. Mint building, features Indian artifacts, nature exhibits, relics of Nevada's early mining days, and a full-scale model of a mine.

Outstanding architecture in the Silver State includes the silver-domed Nevada State Capitol building in Carson City, begun in 1870. The Bowers Mansion and others in nearby Virginia City house valuable antiques brought to this country from many foreign lands. The popular Fleischmann Planetarium, on the Reno campus of the University of Nevada, won a national prize for architecture.

In Las Vegas, the fabulous "Strip" and downtown "Casino Center" are famous for their lavishly designed resort hotel-casinos. Nearby Hoover Dam is, in itself, a giant work of art. Its walkways, walls, and tunnels are filled with treasured Art Deco fixtures and designs, as well as Indian art.

ENTERTAINMENT

A familiar sound in Nevada's cities is the whirl and clink of the one-armed bandits, the popular name for slot machines. Adults over the age of twenty-one gamble their coins in the slot machines at airports and bus terminals, restaurants, grocery stores, even gas stations. Opulent casinos found in cities throughout the state

Las Vegas, with its glittering casino-hotels and spectacular shows, has been called the "Entertainment Capital of the World."

feature other forms of gaming as well, including video poker and such table games as blackjack and roulette. All are open around the clock, and their signs create a wild spectrum of colors that flash, blink, zoom, spiral—everything, in short, but stand still.

Nevada's major nightclubs feature million-dollar spectaculars, star entertainers, ice shows, and Broadway musicals and plays, as well as numerous smaller productions. Some of the shows cost more than $10 million to produce and have casts of more than a hundred performers. Stage effects range from fiery earthquakes to rainstorms with sinking ships, and audiences may find octopuslike stages swinging out over their heads. Bally's in Reno has the world's biggest stage.

The largest resort hotels in Nevada have swimming pools, bowling alleys, movie theaters, video arcades, and plenty of entertainment for those under twenty-one.

SPORTS AND RECREATION

Nevadans like a good contest—whether it be hollering, fiddling, arm wrestling, or left-handed nail driving. And they'll race just about anything: not only automobiles and horses, but hydroplanes and hot-air balloons, Roman-style chariots, and—in Virginia City—even camels and ostriches.

In almost every county, there are fairs and Basque festivals. The National Basque Festival, held in Elko, features sheep-shearing competitions, contests of strength, and colorful dancing. Reno hosts the Nevada State Fair, with a smorgasbord of lively entertainment, interesting exhibits, good food, and fireworks.

Nevada is the home of some of the biggest and most traditional rodeos in the West, where performers test their skills at calf roping, bull riding, steer wrestling, and the like. National rodeo finals are held in Las Vegas, as is the wild western "Helldorado."

The All-Indian Stampede and Rodeo, held annually in Fallon, is one of many "powwows" held throughout the state. At these Indian gatherings, members of various tribes exchange news, trade arts and crafts, and feast and dance together. Authentic buckaroos recite their verses to thousands of admirers at the annual Cowboy Poetry Gatherings in Elko, known as the "Cowboy Poetry Capital of the World."

Nevada offers a full array of sports at the collegiate level. The state has two popular basketball teams, the "Runnin' " Rebels of the University of Nevada-Las Vegas and the Wolf Pack of the Reno campus. In the 1980s, the Rebels advanced to the National Collegiate Athletic Association (NCAA) Tournament seven years in a row, and in 1990, the tenacious team finally won the coveted championship when it beat Duke University by a stunning thirty points.

Beyond its bright lights, Nevada has two national forests spread over widely separated areas. Four such areas make up the Toiyabe National Forest; five areas comprise the Humboldt National Forest. In 1986, Great Basin National Park, Nevada's first, was

created out of more than 77,000 acres (31,161 hectares) of
wilderness in White Pine County.

Nevada has nineteen state parks and monuments. The state
offers outdoor camping, hiking, year-round water sports, and
hunting seasons for deer, duck, and small game. During fishing
season, anglers catch a variety of trout and bass in the state's lakes
and reservoirs. Hang gliding, land sailing, and mountain climbing
are favorite sports in Nevada's open spaces.

One of the finest ski centers in America is in the Reno-Lake
Tahoe area. In the days of the Comstock Lode, a giant of a
Norwegian, "Snowshoe" Thompson, became Nevada's first skier
and the only mail carrier to conquer the snowbound winter
Sierra. Thompson made 10-foot- (3-meter-) long skis and climbed
the mountains with a mailbag on his back that weighed up to
80 pounds (36 kilograms). He made the 180-mile (290-kilometer)
round trip between Genoa, Nevada, and Placerville, California, in
three to five days with neither overcoat nor blanket, traveling day
and night. It was said that he never lost his way through the deep
forests or the wildest of storms. His grave in Genoa has become a
shrine to modern skiers.

Chapter 10
A BRIEF TOUR OF NEVADA

A BRIEF TOUR OF NEVADA

Just beyond Nevada's glittering casinos and resorts lie vast expanses of land—scattered with sprawling ranches, small isolated communities, ghost towns, and panoramic views. Nevada presents its many points of interest in five unique "territories."

RENO-TAHOE TERRITORY

The majestic presence of the Sierra Nevada at the state's western boundary gives the Reno-Tahoe area much of its character. Here was the beginning of the Silver State's history: the first settlement at what is now Genoa and the fabulous Comstock Lode.

Virginia City, surrounded on all sides by rugged hills and rocky mountain peaks, was once the most important city between Denver and San Francisco. Today, the "Liveliest Ghost Town in the West" is a small community of 1,200 residents, outnumbered each year by 1.5 million visitors. Virginia City retains the Comstock flavor in its restored mansions, mines, churches, and the famous Piper's Opera House. Along the creaky wooden boardwalks, the doors still swing at such saloons as the Bucket of Blood and the Silver Queen. Mark Twain's desk stands in the *Territorial Enterprise* building, and the original Virginia & Truckee Railroad carries tourists halfway to Gold Hill and back. Reno is a half-hour drive away.

The most important city in northern Nevada today, Reno started out as a dusty, roughneck town that was the transcontinental railhead for the mines. In 1927, some sixty years

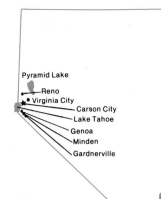

Many buildings
from the mining-boom
era are preserved in
Virginia City, the
"Liveliest Ghost
Town in the West."

after its founding, an iron arch erected across Virginia Street
during the Transcontinental Highways Exposition proclaimed
proudly that Reno was "The Biggest Little City in the World."
Besides offering round-the-clock gaming and one of the best
rodeos in the West, Reno is a cultural mecca and the home of the
University of Nevada. Away from the crowded hotels and casinos,
the city maintains many lovely green parks.

Carson City, one of the nation's smallest state capitals, was
named for renowned scout Kit Carson. Founded as a trading post
in 1858, the city's prime location made it a hub during the gold
and silver strikes of the mid-1800s. Today, much of downtown
Carson City remains in its original state, and many fine examples
of Victorian architecture line its streets.

South of Carson City, the communities of Gardnerville and
Minden form the center of several large ranching operations.
Green meadows and well-tended farms dot the lush Carson Valley
at the foot of the Sierra Nevada.

One of the most popular attractions in the West is dazzlingly
beautiful Lake Tahoe, which Nevada shares with California.
Cupped in the summits of the high Sierra, Lake Tahoe is the

largest and second-deepest alpine lake in North America. Its water is as clear today as it was when Mark Twain wrote, "... where it was only twenty or thirty feet deep the bottom was so perfectly distinct that the boat seemed floating in the air!"

In addition to offering water sports and some of the world's finest cross-country and downhill ski areas, Tahoe has its own exciting hotel-casinos and top-notch entertainment. On the north shore of the lake is Ponderosa Park, a re-creation of the set used in the popular television series "Bonanza."

In contrast to Lake Tahoe, Pyramid Lake—which lies northeast of Reno—comes as a surprise amid the sandy, sage-covered hills that surround it. The lake is part of the Pyramid Lake Indian Reservation and is the only habitat of the cui-ui, a protected species of fish that originated some 2 million years ago.

COVERED-WAGON TERRITORY

Mostly rural and sparsely populated, this region is comprised of three northern Nevada counties: Elko, Humboldt, and Pershing. From the 1840s through the 1860s, thousands of pioneers followed the Humboldt River west. Many graves along the Humboldt, and mounds of abandoned belongings, testified to the dangers of the trail. Today, stunning scenery and a wide range of outdoor recreation draw travelers to this part of Nevada.

The Ruby Range and the East Humboldt Range in northeastern Nevada are the wettest mountains in the Great Basin. In contrast to the vast deserts of the region, the snow-covered peaks of the beautiful Rubies rise more than 11,000 feet (3,353 meters). Several small natural lakes and trout streams attract fishermen, and helicopter skiing in the Rubies has become a popular winter sport. Helicopters take skiers to the pure unspoiled snow at the top of

The scenic Ruby
Range attracts
both skiers and
horseback riders.

the mountains, where the skiing—and the views—are spectacular.

The most important town in northeastern Nevada is Elko, once
called the ''Last Cow Town in the West.'' For years, Elko was a
quiet ranching community and casino stop-off for travelers en
route to Salt Lake City. Then, in 1987, new mining methods made
it possible to glean the submicroscopic particles of gold in the
area. Elko's population soared from ten thousand in 1987 to
sixteen thousand in 1988, making it Nevada's fourth-largest city.
Oldtimers complain that there are too many fast-food joints and
not nearly enough cowboys. But the town's lifestyle still reflects
ranching in one form or another.

Jarbridge, the most isolated of Nevada's ghost towns, lies
102 miles (164 kilometers)—only half of them paved—north of
Elko. The nation's last stagecoach robbery took place in Jarbridge
Canyon during a blizzard in 1916. A handful of people live in the
town today, but hunters fill its few remaining saloons during deer
season.

The National Basque Festival is held every year in Elko.

The 125-mile (201-kilometer) drive west from Elko to Winnemucca is an experience in wide-open spaces. The surrounding mountains rise against azure skies as dramatically as any row of skyscrapers, but can be dwarfed by masses of rolling, ever-changing clouds.

Winnemucca, once called French Ford, lies on the south bank of the Humboldt River. The best view of this crooked, meandering stream, one of North America's longest rivers, can be seen just outside Winnemucca. Once a major stop for wagon trains traveling westward, Winnemucca is a neat, clean, friendly town.

North of Winnemucca lies Paradise Valley, whose green fields and clear streams drew early farmers and ranchers. In the 1870s, mining discoveries in the nearby hills brought brief prosperity to the town. Today, cattle still graze in Paradise Valley and, as in much of the rest of Nevada, have the right-of-way. A tiny population keeps Paradise Valley from becoming a ghost town. Many of the old buildings are still standing, and in one of them, a cottonwood tree has grown through the front wall.

To the southwest, between Winnemucca and Lovelock, is Unionville, a desert oasis in a remote, stream-watered canyon. A dozen families live in this once-thriving mining community, which is the site of a cabin built and lived in by Mark Twain.

Lovelock was a critical stop for pioneers following the Humboldt. The Big Meadows, where the town arose, was the last place where travelers could find abundant grass to feed their stock before crossing the Forty-Mile Desert. Lovelock has the only round courthouse in use in the country. Outside town are the ancient Lovelock Caves and tufa formations created thousands of years ago by prehistoric Lake Lahontan.

PONY EXPRESS TERRITORY

The original—and dangerous—Pony Express route paralleled what is now U.S. Highway 50. *Life* magazine called the stretch of Highway 50 from Ely to Fallon the "loneliest road in America." As a tongue-in-cheek response, residents along the way sponsored an "I Survived Highway 50" campaign, awarding bumper stickers to motorists who drive the entire route.

Today it is more exhilarating than dangerous to drive across central Nevada. With small communities few and far between, and the sight of other vehicles a rarity, the drive resembles a great roller coaster ride up over a series of majestic mountains and down across wide valley floors.

The main attraction for visitors to "Pony Express Territory" is Great Basin National Park. Located at the eastern edge of central Nevada, the park has miles of hiking trails and one of the world's largest groves of ancient bristlecone pine trees. The oldest known living things, bristlecones have a lifespan that can exceed four thousand years.

Great Basin National Park (left) has one of the world's largest groves of ancient bristlecone pines (above).

Also in the park are the Lehman Caves, actually one limestone cave with fascinating rooms extending deep inside the Snake Range. Nearby Wheeler Peak is the summit of the Snake Range and the second-highest peak in Nevada, rising 13,058 feet (3,980 meters).

About an hour's drive from Great Basin National Park, visitors can ride the "Ghost Train of Old Ely," the railroad that once carried ore and passengers for the Kennecott Copper Company. Ely started out as a quiet ranch and stagecoach stop and became, for a time, the center of one of the country's major copper mining regions. It is the hub of commerce and business for much of eastern Nevada, and the surrounding area offers some of the best hunting, fishing, and camping in the state.

West of Ely are Eureka and Austin, two historic mining towns that have scarcely changed since the early 1900s. The 70 miles (113 kilometers) between them were a hard day's gallop for Pony

Express riders and a grueling day's journey by the Overland Stage. Today, travelers on America's "loneliest road" can drive the 120 miles (193 kilometers) from Austin to Fallon in just a few hours. Fallon is the home of the Churchill County Museum, one of the best rural museums in the state. Visitors arriving in the Fallon area can see why it is called the "Oasis of Nevada." The town and the surrounding countryside are green with lawns and trees and many small farms.

Founded in 1902, Fallon blossomed when the first federal reclamation project in the country brought irrigation to the land. The Lahontan Dam, 18 miles (29 kilometers) west of Fallon, was completed in 1915. Nearby Fallon Naval Air Station is one of the top pilot-training schools in the country. Part of the movie *Top Gun* was filmed in the area.

PIONEER TERRITORY

Four counties, comprising more than 20,000 square miles (51,800 square kilometers), make up Nevada's "Pioneer Territory"—the south-central part of the state. This largely uninhabited region contains hundreds of ghost towns or nearly deserted mining camps—including Belmont, Rawhide, and Aurora, which once rivaled Virginia City. All followed the typical boom-and-bust pattern of the early mining towns.

Tonopah sprang to life in 1900, and Goldfield followed soon after. Both started out as collections of tents, shanties, and dugouts. Goldfield became one of the biggest cities in the state, boasting the fanciest hotel between Kansas City, Missouri, and San Francisco. But after boom and bust, floods and fire, little remained of the town. Many historic ruins, including the partially restored Goldfield Hotel, recall the town's glory days.

Tonopah has managed to survive its numerous ups and downs. At least 120 buildings remain from the early 1900s, amid modern gas stations, motels, and convenience stores. With fewer than five thousand residents, Tonopah is still the largest town between Reno and Las Vegas, and a strategic pit stop for travelers. Beneath the town are 350 miles (563 kilometers) of old mining tunnels, and above it, F-117 Stealth fighter planes—with their strange, batlike wings—can be seen flying. The United States Air Force acknowledged in 1989 that it had been working on the secret fighter plane at the nearby Tonopah Test Range.

Between Tonopah and Las Vegas is Beatty, home of a thousand desert dwellers. In the early 1900s, Beatty called itself the "Chicago of the West" because of its importance as a shipping terminal for mining camps in nearby Rhyolite. Today, it is better known for its proximity to the Nevada Test Site and as a gateway to Death Valley. A drive through Titus Canyon takes travelers into the strange beauty of Death Valley National Monument, part of which lies within Nevada's borders.

In the center of the state is Berlin-Ichthyosaur State Park, an unusual combination of ghost town and prehistoric dig. The park contains the remnants of the small mining town of Berlin, abandoned more than seventy-five years ago, and the fossil remains of a number of ichthyosaurs. These huge swimming reptiles, or "fish lizards," grew to 75 feet (23 meters) in length and flourished 70 to 180 million years ago. Their fossil bones lie in what was once a seabed, heaved upward to 7,000 feet (2,134 meters) by volcanic eruptions and violent changes in the earth.

In Lincoln County, between the Utah border and the Nevada Test Site, residents can still gaze across vast valleys at distant mountain ranges with nothing to hinder their view. Though larger than the state of Maryland, Lincoln County has fewer than

Las Vegas is Nevada's chief tourist attraction.

four thousand people. Five of Nevada's nineteen state parks, including Cathedral Gorge, lie in Lincoln County. Two of its towns, Pioche and Panaca, present a classic Nevada contrast: the rough mining city up in the mountains, and the slow, steady farming community in the valley below.

The "Million-Dollar" Courthouse still stands as a reminder that Pioche was once one of the richest and wildest towns in the West. Panaca, established in 1864, has changed little over the last century, with no boom or bust cycles to disturb its quiet routine.

LAS VEGAS TERRITORY

In 1855, a missionary wrote: "We found Las Vegas to be a nice patch of grass about a half a mile wide and two or three miles long. . . ." People who traveled the Old Spanish Trail stopped at *las vegas*, "the meadows," because it was a good camping spot

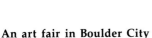
An art fair in Boulder City

with artesian springs. The area, which soon became the site of a Mormon settlement, was destined to grow into the largest city in Nevada, with more than sixty thousand hotel and motel rooms to accommodate visitors from all over the world.

On the campus of the University of Nevada at Las Vegas, a 38-foot (12-meter), 74,000-pound (33,566-kilogram) flashlight was erected in 1981. Its sculptor, Claes Oldenburg, remembered flying over Las Vegas and seeing the city as "a small patch of light in a vast desert darkness." Oldenburg felt a flashlight was "the proper symbol for that beacon of light in the desert."

Las Vegas glitters at the center of southern Nevada's Clark County. Outside the world-famous Las Vegas Strip is a fast-growing suburban community, and beyond the metropolitan area is a superb system of parks and lakes. Mount Charleston towers nearly 12,000 feet (3,658 meters) above sea level, and nearly 10,000 feet (3,048 meters) above the Las Vegas Valley, in sharp contrast to the desert landscape.

An hour's drive from Las Vegas is Nevada's largest state park.

The 40,000-acre (16,188-hectare) Valley of Fire is a startling expanse of red sandstone that has been carved by wind and rain over the years into strange and wonderful shapes. Petrified logs scattered throughout the region indicate that forests once covered the land. Ancient petroglyphs—rock art carved into the cliffs—are reminders of the Pueblo and Basket Maker peoples who once camped here.

Archaeologists explored the famous Lost City (also called Pueblo Grande de Nevada) before it was covered by the waters of Lake Mead in the 1930s. Remnants of ancient Indian life and a reconstructed pueblo can be seen at the Lost City Museum, near Overton, in the Moapa Valley. Also in the Moapa Valley are some Mormon farming communities that are among the oldest continuously cultivated areas of Nevada.

Lake Mead National Recreational Area, located in both Nevada and Arizona, is the largest recreation area in the country. Backed by Hoover Dam, it includes both Lake Mead, created by the dam, and Lake Mohave. Even with some 8 million visitors a year, the area is so vast that at times it appears to be empty. Lakes Mead and Mohave have more than 700 miles (1,127 kilometers) of shoreline and are internationally known sport fisheries.

Near the magnificent Hoover Dam is Boulder City, originally created to house the four thousand workers who built the dam. "Clean, green Boulder City" has become a haven for artists and is the only city in Nevada that does not allow gambling.

Out of a challenging desert-mountain setting, Nevada has carved a unique place for itself in American history. Much of Nevada's past lives on in the present. Its future will depend upon the same kind of hardy spirit that accepted Nevada's challenge and learned to prosper amid its rugged splendor.

FACTS AT A GLANCE

GENERAL INFORMATION

Statehood: October 31, 1864, thirty-sixth state

Origin of Name: *Nevada* is a Spanish word meaning ''snowy'' or ''snow-clad''; the name refers to the snowcapped mountains in the west-central part of the state.

State Capital: Carson City, since 1864

State Nicknames: ''Silver State''; also known as ''Sagebrush State'' and ''Battle Born State''

State Flag: Nevada's flag has a cobalt blue background. A white star lies in the upper left corner. Around the star, clockwise from the top, are the letters N E V A D A. Above the star is a yellow ribbon with the phrase ''Battle Born,'' which refers to the state's entry into the Union during the Civil War. Below the star, two sprigs of sagebrush form a half wreath.

State Motto: All for Our Country

State Bird: Mountain bluebird

State Animal: Desert bighorn sheep

State Flower: Sagebrush

State Tree: Single-leaf piñon

State Song: ''Home Means Nevada,'' words and music by Bertha Raffetto:

> Way out in the land of the setting sun,
> Where the wind blows wild and free,
> There's a lovely spot, just the only one
> That means home, sweet home, to me.
> If you follow the old Kit Carson trail
> Until desert meets the hills,
> Oh, you certainly will agree with me
> It's the place of a thousand thrills.

Home, means Nevada.
Home, means the hills.
Home, means the sage and the pines.

Out by the Truckee's silvery rills,
Out where the sun always shines,
There is a land that I love the best,
Fairer than all I can see.
Right in the heart of the golden west,
Home, means Nevada to me.

POPULATION

Population: 800,493, forty-third among the states (1980 census)

Population Density: 7 people per sq. mi. (3 people per km²)

Population Distribution: 81 percent of the people live in cities or towns. This figure does not mean, however, that Nevada has many big cities, because only Las Vegas and Reno have more than 100,000 people. The main reason the state is so sparsely populated is that more than 85 percent of Nevada's land is owned by the federal government, and is unavailable for development.

Las Vegas	164,674
Reno	100,756
North Las Vegas	42,739
Sparks	40,780
Carson City	32,022
Henderson	24,363
Boulder City	9,590
Elko	8,758

(Population figures according to 1980 census)

Population Growth: For years, Nevada reigned as the nation's least populous state. The empty, unworkable land and the often inhospitable climate deterred many would-be residents. A silver boom brought thousands of prospectors in the 1860s, but most left when the boom was over. The growth of the tourist industry in Las Vegas and Reno, as well as the advent of air conditioning, which made summers more bearable, helped make Nevada one of the fastest-growing states. Its population increased by more than 63 percent from 1970 to 1980, the largest growth rate in the nation. Still, the state has only two major areas of population: the Las Vegas area in the far southern end of Nevada, and the area containing Reno, Sparks, and Carson City in the far western part of the state.

The Colorado River near Las Vegas

Year	Population
1860	6,857
1880	62,266
1900	42,335
1920	77,407
1940	110,247
1950	160,083
1960	285,278
1970	488,738
1980	800,493

GEOGRAPHY

Borders: Nevada is bordered by Idaho and Oregon on the north, California on the west and southwest, and Arizona and Utah on the east.

Highest Point: Boundary Peak in Esmeralda County, 13,143 ft. (4,006 m)

Lowest Point: Colorado River in Clark County, 470 ft. (143 m)

Pyramid Lake is a remnant of an ancient glacial lake that once covered much of western Nevada.

Greatest Distances: North to south—478 mi. (769 km)
East to west—318 mi. (512 km)

Area: 110,540 sq. mi. (286,299 km²)

Rank in Area Among the States: Seventh

Rivers: Nevada's rivers hardly moisten the state's dry landscape. Most would be considered streams in other states. The 300-mi. (483-km) Humboldt, the state's longest river, crosses northern Nevada. The Truckee, originating in Lake Tahoe, flows through Reno. The fast-moving Colorado River, dammed by Hoover Dam, forms Nevada's southeast border. Other rivers include the Carson, Walker, and Virgin. Few of Nevada's rivers make their way to the sea. Most evaporate during the dry season from July to November, leaving behind salty mud flats.

Lakes: Lake Tahoe, a beautiful, large, alpine lake, is a sapphirelike jewel on the Nevada-California border. It is one of the major tourist spots in the West. It is not Nevada's largest lake, however. That honor goes to Lake Mead, on the Arizona border, which was formed by Hoover Dam. Lake Mead measures 247 sq. mi. (640 km²). Pyramid Lake, at 169 sq. mi. (438 km²), is the state's largest natural lake. It was part of a glacial lake known as Lake Lahontan, which once covered some 8,450 sq. mi. (21,886 km²).

Topography: Nevada can be divided into three topographical regions. Most of Nevada lies in the Great Basin, a huge region that extends into Oregon, California, Utah, Wyoming, and Idaho. The name is misleading because it is not a large

The Sierra Nevada reaches into southwestern Nevada.

depression of land, but rather a desert that has the unique characteristic of internal drainage. Within Nevada, this area is known as the Basin and Range Region. A desert area striped by more than thirty north-to-south mountain ranges, it covers all of Nevada except for small areas in the southwestern and northeastern corners of the state.

The Sierra Nevada, the highest range in the lower forty-eight states, reaches into a small southwestern corner of Nevada. Lake Tahoe and other scenic mountain lakes may be found here.

A small pocket of land at the Nevada-Idaho border is part of a region known as the Columbia Plateau. Streams and rivers cut deep canyons here. Lava bedrock lies beneath the region.

Climate: The Sierra Madre to the west blocks many rain clouds from the Pacific Ocean, leaving Nevada the driest state in the nation. Nearly half the state has a desert climate.

Nevada receives an average of about 9 in. (23 cm) of precipitation per year. Southern regions receive the least precipitation. Some western mountains receive heavy snowfall.

Temperatures may vary widely within the state during the same season. Las Vegas, at the far southern end of the state, sees an average temperature of 43° F. (6° C) in January and 90° F. (32° C) in July. Reno, in the western mountains, has an average January temperature of 30° F. (-1° C) in January and 68° F. (20° C) in July. Temperatures in Nevada also vary widely from season to season. Nevada's highest temperature, 122° F. (50° C), was recorded three times: at Leeland on August 12 and 18, 1914, and at Overton on June 23, 1954. The lowest temperature ever recorded in Nevada, -50° F. (-46° C), occurred at San Jacinto on January 8, 1937.

Above: Wildflowers on Wheeler Peak
Right: A blacktailed jackrabbit

NATURE

Trees: Junipers, firs, pines, alders, aspens, cottonwoods, hemlocks, spruces, willows, Joshua trees

Wild Plants: Cactus, yucca, sagebrush, creosote, mesquite, blackbrush, shadscale, greasewood, iodine bush, bitterbrush, squaw apple, cliff rose, serviceberry, hopsage, snowbrush, chokecherry, mistletoe, rye, wheatgrass, bluegrass, larkspurs, lupines, wild carrots, mule ears, geraniums, bluebells

Animals: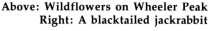 Mule deer, pronghorn antelopes, bighorn sheep, jackrabbits, chipmunks, gophers, mice, lizards, snakes, horned toads, wild horses, burros, elks, skunks, foxes, badgers, beavers, muskrats, minks, porcupines, bobcats, marmots, coyotes, geckos, Gila monsters, mountain lions

Birds: Hummingbirds, eagles, ducks, geese, pelicans, partridges, grouse, quail, rail, snipes, doves, wild turkeys, sage hens, Chinese pheasants

Fish: Trout, black bass, sucker, carp, crappie, bluegill, sunfish, killfish

Left: a golden eagle
Above: Wild horses in the Nevada desert

GOVERNMENT

The government of Nevada, like that of the United States, is divided into three branches. The legislative branch makes laws. Nevada's legislature is divided into a twenty-one-member senate and a forty-two-member assembly. Senators serve four-year terms; assemblymen serve two-year terms. The legislature meets in odd-numbered years, in sessions that last four to six months.

Nevada's governor and lieutenant governor head the executive branch, which enforces the laws. Both serve four-year terms. The secretary of state, treasurer, attorney general, and controller also are elected to four-year terms. The governor appoints the directors and members of more than 150 state bureaus, commissions, and administrative boards.

The judicial branch (court system) interprets laws. Nevada's supreme court has five justices, each elected for six-year terms. It also has nine district courts, as well as a system of local justice courts, small-claims courts, and municipal courts.

Number of Counties: 16, plus one independent city (Carson City)

U.S. Representatives: 2

Electoral Votes: 4

Voting Qualifications: Citizen of the United States, at least eighteen years of age, and resident of Nevada at least thirty days

The Governor's Mansion in Carson City

EDUCATION

Education has always been an important concern in Nevada. One of the state's first actions was the creation, in 1865, of school districts throughout the state. Thus children could receive education even in the most sparsely settled areas.

The entire state of Nevada contains fewer schools than many large eastern cities. There are about 53 high schools, 27 junior high schools, 15 middle schools, 194 elementary schools, and 10 special schools. All children between the ages of seven and seventeen are required to attend school.

The state-run University of Nevada has two campuses, one in Reno and one in Las Vegas. The university also includes the renowned Desert Research Institute and the Mackay School of Mines in Reno, plus a number of community colleges throughout the state. Sierra Nevada College, in Incline Village, is a private liberal-arts school.

ECONOMY AND INDUSTRY

Principal Products:
Agriculture: Cattle, sheep, alfalfa hay, barley, oats, wheat, potatoes, onions, cotton, fruits, vegetables, dairy products, tomatoes, hay, corn, poultry, grapes

Manufacturing: Electronics, printing, publishing, trucking and warehousing, food processing, metal products, industrial chemicals, clothing, and stone, clay, and glass products
Natural Resources: Gold, silver, copper, turquoise, opals, gypsum, limestone, clay, rock, petroleum, natural gas, iron, mercury, lead, zinc, perlite, antimony, tungsten, molybdenum, lithium, diatomite, stone, sand, beryllium, fluorspar, manganese, magnesite, sulfur, waterpower, timber

Business and Trade: Tourism plays a major role in Nevada's economy. Some 44 percent of the state's work force have jobs in the hotel, gaming, and recreation industry. This industry accounts for up to 80 percent of the state's revenue. Nevada has the nation's highest percentage of people working in service jobs.

The federal government, which owns most of Nevada's land, is also one of the state's major employers. Nellis Air Force Base, near Las Vegas, and Fallon Naval Air Station, in the northern part of the state, employ thousands of military personnel.

Warehousing is another important part of the state's economy. A central location between California and the Rocky Mountain states gives Nevada quick access to the rest of the West. In 1949, the state legislature passed a law giving tax exemptions for goods stored briefly in Nevada. The Reno-Sparks area has most of the state's warehouses.

Nevada is one of the least industrialized states. Manufacturing accounts for only a small portion of the state's economy. Most industries in the state are small. A harsh climate prevents Nevada from being a major agricultural state. Livestock products (beef, sheep, poultry, dairy products) are the most important sources of farm income. Nevada has about 2,400 farms and ranches. Most are small, but the largest cover more than 275,000 acres (111,290 hectares).

Communication: Nevada's first mining boom gave rise to the state's first newspaper, the *Territorial Enterprise* of Genoa, founded in 1858. Today, the largest of the more than fifty Nevada newspapers and periodicals are found in the major cities. The largest daily newspapers are the *Las Vegas Review-Journal* and the *Reno Gazette-Journal.*

Nevada has about twenty-eight AM and thirty-six FM radio stations, and about ten television stations. KOH of Reno, the state's oldest radio station, first broadcast in 1928. Nevada's first television stations, KOLO-TV in Reno and KLAS-TV in Las Vegas, started in 1953.

Transportation: Railroads helped Nevada grow. The transcontinental rail system, established in the 1860s, helped create towns out of little more than desert. Today, some 1,600 mi. (2,575 km) of track cross the state. The Union Pacific and Southern Pacific are the most important freight haulers. Amtrak trains carry passengers through the state.

Nevada has about 50,000 mi. (80,465 km) of roads and highways, one-third of them surfaced. Nine federal highways crisscross the state, including Interstate 80 in the northern part of the state and Interstate 15 in the southeastern corner.

In a state with such vast distances between towns, air travel is often a necessity. Nevada has about sixty public and sixty private airports. Reno-Cannon and McCarran International in Las Vegas are the state's largest airports.

Skilled performers participate in the Reno Rodeo, held annually in June.

SOCIAL AND CULTURAL LIFE

Museums: Museums scattered throughout Nevada reflect the diversity of the state. The Nevada State Museum in Carson City houses Indian artifacts, natural-history exhibits, and life-sized mining exhibits built in tunnels beneath the building. Also in Carson City is the Nevada State Railroad Museum, which preserves original equipment from the historic Virginia & Truckee Railroad; and the Stewart Indian Museum, which offers fine exhibits about the history and culture of Nevada's Indian tribes.

The Mackay School of Mines Museum in Reno features displays on mining, mineralogy, and geology. Also in Reno are the Nevada Historical Society Museum, which invites visitors to see cowboy gear, Indian crafts, and early furniture; the William F. Harrah National Automobile Museum, which showcases antique and vintage cars; and the Sierra Nevada Museum of Art, which provides changing exhibits of local, national, and international artists. An atmospherium and the Fleischmann Planetarium brighten the Reno campus of the University of Nevada, and the Las Vegas campus boasts a fine museum of natural history.

Las Vegas's Nevada State Museum and Historical Society is an enjoyable place to study Mojave and Spring Mountains ecology, southern Nevada history, and local art. The Las Vegas Museum of Natural History features life-sized, animated dinosaurs and displays describing the plant and animal life of the Southwest. Other museums in Las Vegas include the Liberace Museum, which exhibits clothing, pianos, and other possessions of the famed pianist; and the Mormon Fort Museum, which honors the early Mormon pioneers.

The Lost City Museum, in Overton, details the lifestyle and culture of the ancient Pueblo Indians who lived in the area. The Clark County Southern Nevada Museum, in Henderson, displays relics from that part of the state. The Nevada Northern Railway Museum, in Ely, preserves the entire old Nevada Northern railyard, including the depot, administration and dispatch office buildings, freight warehouse, machine shops, yard, and miles of track. Among Nevada's many other interesting museums are the Churchill County Museum in Fallon, considered one of the best small museums in Nevada; the Northeastern Nevada Museum in Elko, which has exhibits on Nevada wildlife and history; the Central Nevada Museum in Tonopah, which focuses on the history of Tonopah and central Nevada; and the Genoa Courthouse Museum.

Libraries: The University of Nevada at Reno boasts the state's largest library. Another large collection of books is housed at the University of Nevada at Las Vegas. The Nevada State Library at Carson City, which serves as the official library for the state government, has an impressive law-book collection. The Mackay School of Mines has a strong collection of books on mining and minerals. Altogether, Nevada has about forty public and special library systems.

Performing Arts: Nevada has a lively tradition of performing arts. Ever since 1860, when the opera house in Virginia City hosted operas and vaudeville shows, Nevada has been known for its entertainment. The Artemis W. Ham Concert Hall at the University of Nevada-Las Vegas hosts an annual series of symphonies, operas, and ballets. Northeastern Nevada Museum in Elko stages occasional theatrical performances. The National Basque Festival in Elko allows visitors to enjoy the colorful music and dancing of this ethnic group. Cowboy poets perform each year at the Cowboy Poetry Gathering in Elko.

Sports and Recreation: Nevada's small population has prevented the establishment of major-league baseball, football, and basketball teams, although Las Vegas enjoys a minor-league baseball team. College basketball reigns in Nevada, however. Sellout crowds cheer the University of Nevada-Las Vegas Rebels and the University of Nevada-Reno Wolf Pack. Sports fans also know Las Vegas as an international boxing capital. Dozens of major championships have been fought there.

Those who love the outdoors thrive on Nevada's vast open spaces. Nevada has two national forests: the four-part Toiyabe National Forest in the central, western, and southern part of the state; and the five-part Humboldt National Forest in the north and east. Great Basin National Park covers more than 77,000 acres (31,161 hectares) near Ely. It includes Lehman Caves, which feature huge limestone caverns with 8,200 ft. (2,499 m) of passageways. Nevada also maintains nineteen state parks that offer camping, hiking, hunting, fishing, climbing, hang gliding, and land sailing. The snowbound Sierra Nevada in the western portion of the state provides outstanding skiing in the Reno-Lake Tahoe area. Excellent sport fishing can be found at Lake Mead and nearby Lake Mohave.

The fossils of huge, sea-dwelling dinosaurs have been uncovered at Berlin-Ichthyosaur State Park.

Historic Sites and Landmarks:

Berlin-Ichthyosaur State Park, near Gabbs, contains the silver-mining ghost town of Berlin as well as fossil remains of ichthyosaurs (huge, fishlike dinosaurs).

Fort Churchill Historical State Monument, near Silver Springs, preserves the adobe remnants of a U.S. Army outpost established in 1860 to protect travelers from hostile Indians who resented the influx of settlers.

Marzen House, in Lovelock, is the restored home of Joseph Marzen, a German-born farmer and rancher who moved to Lovelock in the 1870s and became the area's major grain and livestock producer.

Mizpah Hotel, in Tonopah, is a 1907 mining-town hotel that has been restored to its original splendor.

Mormon Station Historic State Monument, in Genoa, displays items from the state's first white settlement.

Rhyolite, near Beatty, is one of Nevada's most picturesque ghost towns.

An old mansion in Virginia City

Virginia City, the "Queen of the Comstock," is a historic mining town that grew up along the Comstock Lode, one of the richest deposits of silver in world history. At its peak in the 1870s, Virginia City was the world's richest mining town. Known as the "World's Liveliest Ghost Town," the town features restored mansions, mine tours, "Old West" saloons, and Piper's Opera House. Nearby *Gold Hill* and *Silver City* also feature historic buildings and sites.

Ward Charcoal Ovens Historic State Monument, near Ely, features ovens that were used to make charcoal for the smelter when the Ward mining camp was booming.

Other Interesting Places to Visit:

Bowers Mansion, near Carson City, was the elaborate home of Sandy and Eilley Bowers, a couple that made, then lost, a fortune in silver mining.

Cathedral Gorge, near Pioche, contains dozens of erosion-carved clay spires that resemble cathedral towers.

Death Valley National Monument, near Beatty, features eerily beautiful landscapes and some of the hottest temperatures in the nation.

Ponderosa Ranch is a re-creation of the set used in the long-running television series "Bonanza."

Hoover Dam, near Boulder City, is an engineering marvel that holds back the mighty Colorado River. It was the largest dam in the world at the time of its completion in 1936.

Lake Tahoe, near Reno, is the largest and second-deepest alpine lake in North America. This deep-blue, crystal-clear lake is the centerpiece of one of the world's finest year-round resorts.

Las Vegas Strip is a colorful array of neon-lit hotels and casinos that run twenty-four hours a day.

Lunar Crater, between Tonopah and Ely, is a vast field of cinder cones and lava that reminded some early visitors of the moon's landscape.

Ponderosa Ranch, on Lake Tahoe, re-creates the set of the popular television show "Bonanza."

Pyramid Lake, near Reno, a starkly beautiful high-desert lake surrounded by rainbow-colored hills, is the remnant of a huge prehistoric lake.

State Capitol, in Carson City, is considered one of the finest examples of Nevada architecture. Built in 1870, it recently underwent a massive, $6-million facelift that restored its original majesty.

Valley of Fire State Park, near Las Vegas, is a wonderland of fiery red sandstone, petrified wood, and Indian petroglyphs.

IMPORTANT DATES

c. 10,000 B.C.—First known people arrive in Nevada

c. 1,000 B.C.—The Lovelock culture, located on the shore of prehistoric Lake Lahontan, flourishes

c. 300 B.C.—The Anasazi ("Ancient Ones") build a thriving civilization near Virgin and Muddy rivers

c. A.D. 1150—The Anasazi leave their homes and fields for reasons still unknown

1776—Francisco Garcés, a Spanish priest, possibly passes through Nevada's southern tip on his way from New Mexico to California, becoming the first European to do so

1821—Mexico wins its independence from Spain, and present-day Nevada consequently becomes part of the Mexican territory

1826—Jedediah Smith becomes the first American to cross present-day Nevada

1828—Peter Skene Ogden, heading a party of Hudson's Bay Company trappers, discovers the Humboldt River

1830—William Wolfskill blazes Old Spanish Trail from Santa Fe to Los Angeles, opening Nevada to trade from the southeast

1833-34—Members of Walker-Bonneville party become the first white men to follow the Humboldt River west

1841—John Bidwell and John Bartleson lead the first successful emigrant crossing of the Great Basin

1843-44—John C. Frémont explores Nevada during a U.S. government-sponsored expedition to the West

1848—U.S. acquires future state of Nevada after winning Mexican War; discovery of gold in California brings travelers through Nevada, although few settle in Nevada

1850—Congress establishes Utah Territory, which includes most of present-day Nevada; Mormon prospectors discover gold in Gold Canyon

1851—Mormon Station (later called Genoa), a trading post built in the Carson Valley by a group of Mormons, becomes Nevada's first non-Indian settlement

1854—The Utah territorial legislature organizes the Carson Valley and surrounding region into Carson County

1855 — Mormons sent by Brigham Young settle Las Vegas

1856 — Brigham Young orders all Mormons to return to Utah to avoid attack by U.S. forces sent out to subdue Mormon resistance to federal rule

1858 — The *Territorial Enterprise*, Nevada's first newspaper, begins publication

1859 — A group of prospectors discover what would prove to be the richest mining region in the world at Gold Hill, near present-day Virginia City; Peter O'Riley and Patrick McLaughlin strike gold and silver nearby, in Ophir Ravine; Henry Comstock claims ownership of their discovery and names it the Comstock Lode; Virginia City grows up almost overnight as prospectors flock to the region

1860 — White settlers defeat Paiutes in the Pyramid Lake War; U.S. Army builds Fort Churchill; Pony Express begins mail delivery, using a route through Nevada

1861 — Congress establishes Nevada Territory; first territorial legislature meets; transcontinental telegraph is completed, making Pony Express obsolete

1863 — First Nevada constitutional convention meets; voters reject proposed constitution

1864 — Nevada enters the Union as the thirty-sixth state; voters ratify state constitution

1865 — State legislature creates first school districts

1866 — Nevada gains some eastern land from Utah Territory

1867 — Nevada gains southern triangle of land from Arizona Territory

1868 — Charles Crocker and Myron C. Lake found Reno

1869 — Thirty-seven miners die in the Yellow Jacket mine disaster

1870 — Masked men steal $40,000 at Verdi (near Reno) in the West's first train robbery; U.S. government opens a mint in Carson City

1873 — John Mackay discovers the "Big Bonanza" silver lode in Virginia City; Mint Act of 1873, limiting the use of silver in U.S. currency, causes a drop in silver prices; this results in the closing of many mines and the decline of many once-lively communities into ghost towns in the 1870s

1874 — The University of Nevada, the state's first university, is opened at Elko; Pyramid Lake and Walker River Indian reservations are established

1875 — Fire destroys most of Virginia City; the mining town never entirely recovers from effects of the blaze

This 1910 photograph shows a Nevada woman standing in front of crops made possible by the Newlands Irrigation Project.

1885—State legislature moves University of Nevada from Elko to Reno

1889—Churchill County Telephone & Telegraph System, today the only county-owned telephone system in the nation, begins operations

1893—Carson City mint closes

1897—Nevada legislature passes a bill allowing prizefights; Robert Fitzsimmons defeats "Gentleman Jim" Corbett in one of the nation's first major fights

1900—James Butler's silver discovery sparks creation of Tonopah

1902—The Newlands Reclamation Act, authored by Nevada politician Francis Newlands, empowers the U.S. government to build dams and irrigation projects in the West

1904—Nevada Progressive politicians pass referendum legislation

1905—A railroad line is built from Salt Lake City to Los Angeles, vitalizing Las Vegas

1907—Industrial Workers of the World (nicknamed the "Wobblies") lead a miners' strike at Goldfield; the Newlands Irrigation Project, the first federal irrigation project, is completed along the Carson and Truckee rivers

Hoover Dam, one of the world's tallest dams, was completed in 1936.

1909—Nevada legislature outlaws all gambling in the state

1918—Nevada senator Key Pittman spearheads Pittman Act, under which federal government agrees to buy a certain amount of Nevada silver

1928—KOH in Reno, Nevada's first radio station, begins broadcasting

1931—State legislature legalizes gambling and reduces divorce residency requirement from three months to six weeks

1932—Federal government builds Boulder City to house Boulder Dam workers

1936—Boulder (later renamed Hoover) Dam, built to control Colorado River at Nevada-Arizona border, is completed

1950—Atomic Energy Commission designates part of the Las Vegas Bombing and Gunnery Range for the testing of nuclear weapons

1951—Nuclear-weapons testing begins at the Nevada Test Site

1954—Petroleum is discovered in Nye County

1963—Nevada Indians establish a statewide tribal council; U.S. Supreme Court specifies how much water Nevada, Arizona, and Colorado may take from the Colorado River

1967—In an attempt to "clean up" the gambling industry, state legislature passes a law allowing corporations that sell stock to the public to own casinos

1969—The state formally establishes University of Nevada system

1971—University of Nevada-Reno opens a medical school

1980—A fire in the MGM Grand hotel in Las Vegas kills eighty-four people

1982—Barbara Vucanovich becomes Nevada's first U.S. congresswoman

1986—Tahoe Regional Planning Agency adopts a master plan to regulate growth in the area for the next twenty years; Great Basin National Park, Nevada's first national park, is established

1988—University of Nevada opens an international division in Tokyo

IMPORTANT PEOPLE

LUCIUS BEEBE

Lucius Beebe (1902-1966), journalist; reestablished the famous Nevada newspaper the *Territorial Enterprise*; wrote *Comstock Commotion; The Story of the Territorial Enterprise*, as well as many stories about trains

Alan Harvey Bible (1909-1989), politician; U.S. senator from Nevada (1954-74); chaired the Interior Appropriations Subcommittee, which determines how to allot money for federal lands projects

WALTER CLARK

SAMUEL CLEMENS

DAT-SO-LA-LEE

JAMES FAIR

Bertha Muzzy (B.M.) Bower (1871-1940), writer; created dozens of western romantic novels, some set in Nevada; wrote under pseudonym B. M. Bower because her publishers feared readers would not take seriously books written by a woman; gained respect for her realistic accounts of the West; wrote *Chip of the Flying U*

Emmet D. Boyle (1879-1926), born in Virginia City; politician; Nevada's first native-born governor (1915-23)

John Ross (J. Ross) Browne (1821-1875), writer; created characters who poked fun at the Comstock silver rush years; wrote *Crusoe's Island, with Sketches and Adventure in Washoe,* and "A Peep at Washoe"

Howard Cannon (1912-   ), politician; U.S. senator from Nevada (1959-83); chairman of influential Senate Commerce Committee

Christopher "Kit" Carson (1809-1868), frontiersman; guided John C. Frémont's expedition through Nevada; became known for his skills as a guide, hunter, and soldier; became brigadier general in U.S. Army

Walter Van Tilburg Clark (1909-1971), writer, teacher; best-known work is the novel *The Ox-Bow Incident*; writer-in-residence at the University of Nevada (1962-71)

Orion Clemens (1825-1897), lawyer, government official; served as territorial secretary of Nevada Territory; his brother Samuel, who later took the pen name Mark Twain, came to work with him in Virginia City

Samuel Langhorne Clemens (1835-1910), writer; using the pen name Mark Twain, became one of America's most famous and beloved authors; created famous characters Tom Sawyer and Huckleberry Finn; came to Nevada in 1861 to serve as his brother's private secretary; wrote stories for the *Territorial Enterprise*; wrote the book *Roughing It* about his adventures in Nevada

Henry Comstock (1820-1870), prospector; claimed ownership of the rich deposit of silver and gold ore in southwestern Nevada that became known as the Comstock Lode

Abby Dalton (1935-   ), born in Las Vegas; actress; appeared in the television programs "Hennesey," "The Joey Bishop Show," and "The Jonathan Winters Show"

Dat-So-La-Lee (?-1925), born in Nevada; Washo Indian basket maker who achieved fame for the quality of her work

James Fair (1831-1894), miner; discovered a massive gold and silver pocket in the Consolidated Virginia Mine; organized Bank of Nevada; held land, building, and railroad interests; U.S. senator from Nevada (1881-87)

John Charles Frémont (1813-1890), explorer; traveled through the Great Basin and Sierra Nevada during a U.S. government-sponsored scientific expedition (some believe it was a spy mission) of the West (1843-45)

Sarah Winnemucca Hopkins (1844?-1891), guide, interpreter, author; granddaughter of Truckee and daughter of Winnemucca; wrote *Life Among the Paiutes: Their Wrongs and Claims*

Howard Robard Hughes (1905-1976), industrialist, aviator, aircraft designer, film producer; in the 1960s, bought land and casinos in and around Las Vegas; spent many years as a recluse in Las Vegas

John P. Jones (1829-1912), miner, politician; made a fortune as a developer of mineral resources in Nevada; U.S. senator from Nevada (1873-1903)

Jack Kramer (1921-   ), born in Las Vegas; professional tennis player; America's top tennis star in the 1940s; won U.S. National championships in 1946 and 1947, British Open in 1947, and four U.S. doubles championships

Paul Laxalt (1922-   ), born in Reno; politician; governor of Nevada (1966-70); U.S. senator from Nevada (1975-87); managed Ronald Reagan's presidential campaigns in 1976 and 1980; advised Reagan on legislative matters during his administration

Robert Laxalt (1923-   ), writer; brother of Paul Laxalt; grew up in Nevada; wrote on Basque history and culture; paid tribute to his immigrant father in his book *Sweet Promised Land*

William P. Lear (1902-1978), inventor; developed the Lear jet, a small private jet; held many mining claims throughout the state

Liberace (1919-1987), born Wladziu Liberace; pianist, entertainer; created lavish entertainment extravaganzas and wore expensive, outlandish wardrobes during his Las Vegas shows and concerts

John William Mackay (1831-1902), miner, businessman; made a fortune after striking rich ore in a section of the Comstock Lode that became known as the "Big Bonanza" (1873); used his money to found Nevada Bank of San Francisco and companies that set up telegraph cable lines in the U.S. and across the Atlantic to Europe; his son, Clarence, donated funds to found the Mackay School of Mines, at the University of Nevada, in his father's honor

Mary McNair Mathews (1834-1903), writer; described her experiences in Virginia City in her book *Ten Years in Nevada; Or, Life on the Pacific Coast*

Patrick Anthony McCarran (1871-1954), born in Reno; politician; U.S. senator from Nevada (1933-54); chairman of the Judiciary Committee; sponsored the Internal Security Act, designed to control Communists, and the McCarran-Walter Act, which tightened control over aliens and immigrants

JOHN C. FRÉMONT

SARAH WINNEMUCCA HOPKINS

LIBERACE

JOHN MACKAY

EMMA NEVADA

FRANCIS NEWLANDS

TASKER ODDIE

KEY PITTMAN

James Nash (1945-   ), born in Hawthorne; professional baseball player; pitched for Kansas City and Oakland Athletics, Atlanta Braves, and Philadelphia Phillies; stunned baseball world with his 12-1 rookie record for the 1966 Kansas City Athletics

Emma Nevada (1859-1946), born Emma Wixon; opera singer; grew up near Austin; appeared in leading opera halls throughout Europe; starred in *The Rose of Sharon*, an opera composed especially for her

Francis Griffith Newlands (1848-1917), politician; U.S. representative from Nevada (1893-1903); U.S. senator (1903-17); led quest for state-owned irrigation and free silver coinage; sponsored the Newlands Reclamation Act (1902), a law requiring that money from sale of public lands be used for irrigation projects; his efforts led to the creation of the U.S. Reclamation Service and the Federal Trade Commission

Wayne Newton (1942-   ), entertainer, hotel owner; inveterate Las Vegas and Reno performer; famous for singing "Danke Schoen" and "Red Roses for a Blue Lady"

George Nixon (1860-1912), financier, politician; made fortune in Nevada silver mines; built Majestic Theater in Reno and Nixon Opera House in Winnemucca; U.S. senator from Nevada (1905-12)

Thelma Catherine (Pat) Nixon (1912-   ), born in Ely; wife of President Richard M. Nixon; served as a quiet, gracious first lady during her husband's administration (1969-74)

James W. Nye (1815-1876), politician; served as Nevada's only territorial governor; helped guide Nevada to statehood; U.S. senator (1864-73)

Tasker Loundes Oddie (1870-1950), politician; governor of Nevada (1911-15); U.S. senator (1921-33)

Peter Skene Ogden (1794-1854), explorer; discovered the Humboldt River while on a hunting expedition for the British-owned Hudson's Bay Company

Sarah Elizabeth Thompson Olds (1875-1963), homesteader, author; built homestead near Twenty Mile House, between Reno and Pyramid Lake; established a local school district; wrote of her homesteading experiences in *Twenty Miles from a Match*

Key Pittman (1877-1940), politician; came to Nevada during the Tonopah-Goldfield rush; U.S. senator (1913-40); served as chairman of Foreign Relations Committee; known as the "Silver Senator" for his advocacy of the use of silver in American currency; championed the Pittman Act (1918), which guaranteed government purchase of silver

Mark Requa (1865-1937), born in Virginia City; mining engineer, political leader; built Nevada Northern Railway; president of Eureka and Palisades Railway; oil director of United States Fuel Administration during Herbert Hoover administration; wrote *Grubstake*, a novel based on his mining experiences

Charles Hinton Russell (1903-), born in Lovelock; politician; governor of Nevada (1951-59); led campaign to curb organized crime's control of the gambling industry

CHARLES RUSSELL

James G. Scrugham (1880-1945), politician; governor of Nevada (1923-27); U.S. representative (1933-42); U.S. senator (1942-45)

William Sharon (1821-1885), financier; managed Virginia City's Bank of California; through the bank, gained control of the most important mills and mines in the state; U.S. senator from Nevada (1875-81)

Benjamin "Bugsy" Siegel (1903-1947), racketeer, hotel owner; opened Flamingo Hotel, which helped Las Vegas become the gambling capital of the United States

Jedediah Smith (1798?-1831), trader, explorer; crossed present-day Nevada while searching for a trade route to California (1826-27)

RICKY SOBERS

Ricky Sobers (1953-), professional basketball player; starred at the University of Nevada-Las Vegas; averaged better than fourteen points per game with Phoenix Suns, Indiana Pacers, and Chicago Bulls

John Sparks (1843-1908), politician, rancher; introduced Hereford cattle to Nevada; governor of Nevada (1903-08); the town of Sparks is named after him

William Morris Stewart (1827-1909), lawyer, politician; served as one of Nevada's first U.S. senators (1864-75, 1887-1905); known for his sponsorship of state and national mining legislation; authored final version of Fifteenth Amendment to the Constitution, which gave black males voting rights (1869); championed Carson City as Nevada capital

WILLIAM STEWART

Adolph Sutro (1830-1898), engineer; developed Sutro Tunnel to provide mine transportation, drainage, and ventilation in the Comstock mines; mayor of San Francisco (1895-97)

Jerry Tarkanian (1930-), basketball coach; directed University of Nevada-Las Vegas Rebels into NCAA basketball tournament many times since 1973; coached fast-paced, high-scoring games that earned his team the nickname "Runnin' Rebels"

ADOLPH SUTRO

BARBARA VUCANOVICH

WOVOKA

Barbara Vucanovich (1921-   ), politician; U.S. representative from Nevada (1982-   ); Nevada's first U.S. congresswoman

John Taylor Waldorf (1870-1932), journalist; edited the *San Francisco Bulletin* for many years; wrote columns describing his youth in Virginia City and an autobiography, *A Kid on the Comstock*

Joseph Walker (1798-1876), explorer; followed Humboldt River from Utah through Nevada; defeated Paiutes in first full-scale battle between whites and Indians in Utah

Sessions Wheeler (1911-   ), born in Fernley; writer, conservationist; wrote the novel *Paiute* and such nonfiction books as *Desert Lake* and *The Nevada Desert*; served on many conservation and Indian affairs boards

George Wingfield (1876-1959), financier; made fortune in Nevada mining operations; owned twelve Nevada banks at time of 1929 stock market crash; served as advisor to Nevada Republican party

Truckee (?-1859), chief of Northern Paiutes; Indian name was Winnemucca, but was nicknamed "Truckee" by white explorers; guided John C. Frémont and several other parties on explorations through Nevada; sought peace between Indians and whites

Winnemucca (1799?-1882), Paiute chief; son of Truckee; succeeded his father as chief of Northern Paiutes; signed treaty with whites to end Pyramid Lake War (1862)

Wovoka (1856?-1932), born in Nevada; Paiute Indian prophet; established the Ghost Dance religious movement in the late 1800s

William Wright (1829-1898), journalist, author; wrote under the pen name Dan DeQuille; reporter for the *Territorial Enterprise*; wrote *The Big Bonanza* and other books

GOVERNORS

Henry G. Blasdel	1864-1871	Richard Kirman, Sr.	1935-1939
Lewis R. Bradley	1871-1879	Edward P. Carville	1939-1945
John H. Kinkead	1879-1883	Vail M. Pittman	1945-1951
Jewett W. Adams	1883-1887	Charles H. Russell	1951-1959
Charles C. Stevenson	1887-1890	Grant Sawyer	1959-1967
Frank Bell	1890-1891	Paul Laxalt	1967-1971
Roswell K. Colcord	1891-1895	Mike O'Callaghan	1971-1979
John E. Jones	1895-1896	Robert List	1979-1983
Reinhold Sadler	1896-1903	Richard H. Bryan	1983-1988
John Sparks	1903-1908	Robert Miller	1988-
Denver S. Dickerson	1908-1911		
Tasker L. Oddie	1911-1915		
Emmet D. Boyle	1915-1923		
James G. Scrugham	1923-1927		
Frederick B. Balzar	1927-1934		
Morley Griswold	1934-1935		

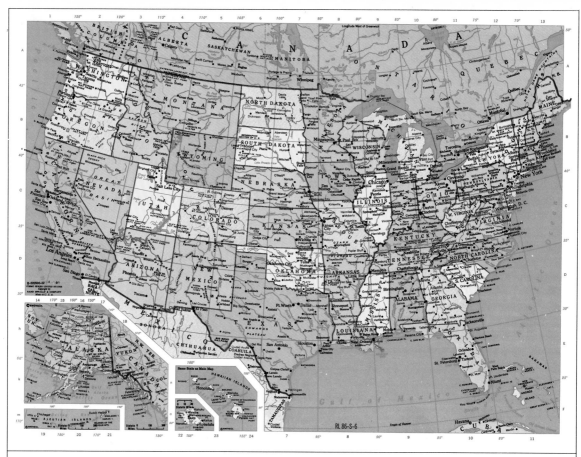

Topography

MAP KEY

Alkali Lake	B2
Amargosa Desert	G5
Antelope Peak	B7
Antelope Range	D7
Arc Dome (mountain)	E4
Ash Springs	F6
Aurora	E3
Austin	D4
Babbitt	E3
Baker	D7
Basalt	E3
Battle Mountain	C5
Battle Mountain Indian Reservation	C4
Beatty	G5
Becky Peak	D7
Belmont Ghost Town	E4
Belted Range	F5
Beowawe	C5
Big Mountain	B2
Big Smoky Valley	E4
Bilk Creek Mountains	B3
Black Rock Desert	C3
Black Rock Range	B3
Black Springs	D2
Blue Diamond	G6
Boulder City	H7
Boundary Peak	F3
Brawley Peaks	E3
Bruneau River	A6
Bull Creek	E6
Bunker Hill (mountain)	D4
Bunkerville	G7
Butte Mountains	D6
Cactus Flat	F5
Cactus Peak	F5
Cactus Springs	G6
Calcutta Lake	B2
Caliente	F7
Capital Peak	B4
Carlin	C5
Carp	F7
Carson City	D2
Carson Lake (dry lake)	D3
Carson River	D2
Carson Sink (dry lake)	D3
Caselton	F7
Cathedral Gorge State Park	F7
Catnip Mountain	B2
Centerville	E2
Charcoal Ovens Historic State Monu.	D7
Charleston Park	G6
Charleston Peak	G6
Christina Peak	D6
Clan Alpine Mountains	D3
Coaldale	E4
Cobre	B7
Coils Creek	D5
Cold Springs	D4
Colorado River	H7
Comstock Lake Mine	D2
Contact	B7
Cortez Mountains	C5
Cottonwood Cove	H7
Crescent Valley	C5
Crooks Lake	B2
Crystal Bay	D1
Currant	D7
Currant Mountain	E6
Davis Dam	H7
Dayton	D2
Deeth	B6
Denio	B3
Desert Creek Peak	E2
Desert Valley	B3
Diamond Mountains	D6
Dixie Valley	D3
Dresslerville	E2
Dry Creek Mountain	B5
Dry Lake	G7
Duck Creek	D7
Duck Valley Indian Reservation	B5
Duckwater	E6
Duckwater Indian Reservation	E6
Duckwater Peak	E6
Duffer Peak	B3
Dunphy	C5
Dyer	F3
East Las Vegas	G6
East Range	C4
East Walker River	E2
Echo Bay	G7
Egan Range	E7
Elgin	F7
Elko	C6
Ely	D7
Empire	C2
Eureka	D6
Excelsior Mountains	E3
Fairview Peak	D3
Fallon	D3
Fallon Indian Reservation	D3
Fallon Naval Air Station	D3
Fernley	D2
Fort Churchill Historic State Monu.	D2
Fort McDermitt Indian Reservation	B4
Fort Mojave Indian Reservation	H7
Fox Mountain	B2
Franklin Lake	C6
Frenchman Lake (dry lake)	G6
Gabbs	E4
Gardnerville	E2
Genoa	D2
Gerlach	C2
Glenbrook	D2
Golconda	C4
Gold Point	F4
Goldfield	F4
Goodsprings	H6
Goose Creek	B7
Goshute Indian Reservation	D7
Goshute Lake (dry lake)	C7
Goshute Mountains	C7
Granite Peak	B4
Granite Peak	C2
Granite Range	C2
Grant Range	E6
Grapevine Peak	G4
Great Basin	
Great Basin Boundary	B5
Great Basin National Park	E7
Groom Lake (dry lake)	F6
Groom Range	F6
Halleck	C6
Hamilton Mountain	D6
Hawthorne	E3
Hayford Peak	G6
Hays Canyon Peak	B2
Haystack Mountain	B6
Hazen	D2
Henderson	G7
Hidden Valley	D2
Hiko	F6
Hiko Range	F6
Hole in the Mountain Peak	C6
Hoover Dam	H7
Hot Creek Range	E5
Hot Creek Valley	E5
Hot Springs Peak	B4
Huffakers	D2
Humboldt	C3
Humboldt Range	C3
Humboldt River	C3
Humboldt River (North Fork)	B3
Huntington Creek	C6
Ichthyosaur Fossil Beds	E4
Imlay	C3
Incline	D2
Independence Mountains	C5
Indian Springs	G6
Ione	E4
Jackpot	B7
Jackson Mountains	B3
Jarbridge	B6
Jean	H6
Jiggs	C6
Job Peak	D3
Jumbo Peak	G7
Kawich Peak	F5
Kawich Range	F5
Kershaw-Ryan Canyon	F7
Keystone	D5
King Lear Peak	B3
Kings River	B3
Lahontan Reservoir	D2
Lake Mead National Recreation Area	H7
Lake Range	C2
Lake Valley	E7
Lakeridge	E2
Lamoille	C6
Lane	D7
Lane Mountain	E4
Las Vegas	G6
Las Vegas Bombing and Gunnery Range	H7
Lathrop Wells	G5
Laughlin	H7
Lee	C6
Lemmon Valley	D2
Lida	F4
Lincoln Park	D2
Little Humboldt River	B4
Little Humboldt River (North Fork)	B4
Little Humboldt River (South Fork)	B5
Little Owyhee River	B5
Logandale	G7
Lovelock	C3
Lower Lake	B2
Lund	E6
Luning	E3
Maggie Creek	C5
Manhattan	E4
Margruder Mountain	F4
Marys River	B6
Mason	E2
Massacre Lake	B2
Matterhorn Mountain	B6
McAfee Peak	B6
McCullough Mountain	H6
McDermitt	B4
McGill	D7
Mead Lake	G7
Meadow Valley Wash	F7
Mesquite	G7
Mill City	C3
Mina	E3
Minden	E2
Moapa	G7
Moapa Indian Reservation	F6
Mohave Lake	H7
Monitor Range	E5
Monitor Valley	E5
Montello	B7
Morey Peak	E5
Mormon Peak	G7
Mormon Station Historic State Monu.	D2
Mount Callaghan	D5
Mount Grant	E3
Mount Irish	F6
Mount Jefferson	E5
Mount Lewis	C5
Mount Montgomery	E3
Mount Moriah	D7
Mount Rose	D2
Mount Tobin	C4
Mount Wilson	E7
Mountain City	B6
Mountain Springs	G6
Mud Lake (dry lake)	F4
Muddy Mountains	G7
Muddy Peak	G7
Nellis Air Force Base	G6
Nelson	H7
New Washoe City	D2
Newark Lake (dry lake)	D6
Nixon	D2
North Las Vegas	G6
North Schell Peak	D7
North Shoshone Peak	D4
Oasis	B7
Oreana	C3
Orovada	B4
Overton	G7
Owyhee	B5
Owyhee River (South Fork)	B5
Owyhee River	B5
Pahrump	G6
Pahute Mesa	F5
Panaca	F7
Pancake Range	E6
Paradise	G6
Paradise Valley	B4
Patsville	B6
Pequop	B7
Pequop Mountains	C7
Pilot Peak	G7
Pilot Peak	E4
Pilot Range	B7
Pine Creek	C5
Pine Forest Range	B3
Pintwater Range	G6
Pioche	F7
Pleasant Valley	D2
Prince	F7
Pyramid Lake	C2
Pyramid Lake Indian Reservation	D2
Quinn Canyon Range	F6
Quinn River	B4
Railroad Valley	E6
Ralston Valley	E4
Reese River	D4
Reno	D2
Rhyolite	G5
Rixie's	C5
Roberts Creek Mountain	D5
Rock Creek	C5
Round Mountain	E4
Ruby Dome (mountain)	C6
Ruby Lake	C6
Ruby Mountains	C6
Ruby Valley	C6
Ruth	D6
Rye Patch Reservoir	C3
Salmon Falls Creek	B7
Santa Rosa Range	B4
Schell Creek Range	E7
Schurz	E3
Seaman Range	F6
Searchlight	H7
Shafter	C7
Sheep Peak	G6
Sheep Range	G6
Shoshone Mountains	E4
Shoshone Peak	G5
Shoshone Range	C5
Silver City	D2
Silver Peak Range	F4
Silver Springs	D2
Silverpeak	F4
Singing Sand Mountain	D3
Skyland	D2
Sloan	H6
Smith	E2
Smoke Creek Desert	C2
Snake Range	E7
Snow Water Lake	C7
Sonoma Peak	C4
Sonoma Range	C4
Sparks	D2
Spring Mountains	G6
Spring Creek	C4
Spruce Mountain	C7
Star Peak	C3
Stateline	H6
Stateline	E2
Steamboat	D2
Steptoe	D7
Stewarts Points	G7
Stillwater	D3
Stillwater Range	D3
Sulphur Spring Range	D5
Summit Lake Indian Reservation	B2
Summit Mountain	D5
Sun Valley	D2
Sunrise Manor	G6
Sutcliffe	D2
Tahoe Lake	D1
Te-Mook Indian Reservation	C6
Tempiute	F6
Thousand Spring Creek	B7
Toano Range	C7
Tobin Range	C4
Tohakum Peak	C2
Toiyabe Range	E4
Tonopah	F5
Topaz Lake	E2
Topaz Ranch Estates	E2
Toquima Range	E5
Tracy Clark	D2
Trident Peak	B3
Trinity Peak	C3
Trinity Range	C3
Troy Peak	E6
Truckee River	D2
Tuscarora	B5
Tuscarora Mountains	C5
Unionville	C4
University of Nevada	D2
Ursine	F7
Valmy	C4
Verdi	D2
Verdi Peak	C6
Virgin Mountains	G7
Virgin River	G8
Virgin River Canyon	G7
Virginia City	D2
Virginia Peak	D2
Vista	D2
Wabuska	D2
Wadsworth	D2
Walker Lake	E3
Walker River	D3
Walker River Indian Reservation	E3
Warm Springs	E5
Washoe City	D2
Wassuk Range	E2
Weed Heights	E2
Wellington	E2
Wells	B7
Wendover	C7
West Walker River	E2
Wheelbarrow Peak	F5
Wheeler Peak	E7
White Mountains	F3
White River	E6
Wild Horse Reservoir	B6
Willow Beach	H7
Willow Creek	E5
Winchester	G6
Winnemucca	C4
Winnemucca Lake (dry lake)	C2
Worthington Peak	F6
Yerington	E2
Yerington Indian Reservation	D2
Yomba Indian Reservation	D4
Yucca Lake (dry lake)	F5
Yucca Mountain	G5
Zephyr Cove	E2

1 120°   2   119°   3   118°   4   117°   5   116°   6   115°   7   114°   8

OREGON   IDAHO

A
42°
FT. BIDWELL IND. RES.   CATNIP MTN. 7294   Denio   McDermitt   FT. McDERMITT IND. RES.   Owyhee   Jarbidge   Jackpot   Yost
Goose L.   Calcutta Lake   Alkali   Massacre L.   TRIDENT PK. 8393   McDERMITT   CAPITOL PK. 8364   DUCK VALLEY IND. RES.   Mountain City   Watterhorn 10839   Contact   RAFT RIVER MTS.   Grouse Creek

B
HAYS CANYON PK. 7916   BIG MTN. 8594   Orovada   Paradise Valley   GRANITE PK. 9732   MC AFEE PK. 10439   HAYSTACK MTN. 8200   Montello   Pequop
SUMMIT LAKE IND. RES.   KING LEAR PK. 8923   HOT SPRINGS PK. 6450   DRY CREEK PK. 8391   ANTELOPE PK. 8788   Lucin
Tuscarora   GREAT   SALT LAKE DESERT

C
41°
FOX MTN. 8182   Winnemucca   Golconda   Deeth   Wells   HOLE IN THE MTN. 11306   PILOT PK. 10716   Shafter
Gerlach   GRANITE PK. 8974   SONOMA PK. 9395   Valmy   Dunphy   Carlin   Elko   Lamoille   Halleck   Wendover
Empire   Humboldt   Mill City   Battle Mountain   Beowawe   TE-MOAK IND. RES.   Lee   VERDI PK. 11024   SPRUCE MTN. 10262   TOOELE
Unionville   RUBY DOME 11387   SNOW WATER L.   DESERT

D
40°
TRINITY PK. 7337   Oreana   MT. TOBIN 9775   MT. LEWIS 9680   Jiggs   Ruby Valley   BECKY PK. 9999   Ibapah
TSHAWHAW PK. 8182   Lovelock   ROBERTS CR. MTN. 10133   Eureka   IBAPAH PK. 12087   GOSHUTE IND. RES.   Trout Creek
Winnemucca L.   Carson Sink   MT. CALLAGHAN 10187   CHRISTINA PK. 9656   Steptoe   Partoun
PYRAMID L. IND. RES.   Nixon   Austin   SUMMIT MTN. 10461   MT. HAMILTON 10745   Ruth   McGill   N. SCHELL PK. 11883   CONFUSION RANGE
Sutcliffe   Virginia Lake   FALLON IND. RES.   JOB PK. 8785   Cold Spgs.   BUNKER HILL 11474   Lane   Ely   MT. MORIAH 12050
VIRGINIA PK. 8367   Fernley   Fallon   Kingston   YOMBA IND. RES.   Baker
Portola   Loyalton   Sun Valley   Wadsworth   Silver Springs   Salt Wells   NORTH SHOSHONE PK. 10313

E
39°
Reno   Sparks   Hazen   Frenchman   Ione   FAIRVIEW PK. 8303   Gabbs   ARC DOME 11773   MT. JEFFERSON 11941   DUCKWATER PK. 9063   WHEELER PK. 13063   GREAT BASIN NAT. PARK   Garrison
Verdi   MT. ROSE 10776   Steamboat   Virginia City   DUCKWATER IND. RES.   Duckwater   CURRANT MTN. 11513   Lund
Truckee   Incline Village   Silver City   Dayton   Round Mountain   MOREY PK. 10246
Washoe City   Carson City   Stewart   Wabuska   MT. GRANT 11239   Bobbitt   Luning   PILOT PK. 9182   Manhattan   MT. TROY PK. 11298   MT. WILSON 9315
Crystal Bay   Skyland   Glenbrook   Genoa   YERINGTON IND. RES.   Yerington   Smith   Wellington   Warm Springs   Pioche   INDIAN PK. 9790
Zephyr Cove   Minden   Gardnerville   Mason   DESERT CR. PK. 8969   Hawthorne   BRAWLEY PKS. 9542   Mina   LONE MTN. 9108   Tonopah   Caselton   Prince

F
38°
Stateline   Dresslerville   MT. PATTERSON 11673   Excelsior   Basalt   Coaldale   KAWICH PK. 9404   WORTHINGTON PK. 8850   Panaca   Modena   Ursine
Markleeville   Topaz L.   Mount Montgomery   Silverpeak   Goldfield   CACTUS PK. 7482   MT. IRISH 8743   Caliente   Enterprise
Coleville   EXCELSIOR MTN. 13446   BOUNDARY PEAK HIGHEST POINT IN NEVADA 13441   Dyer   CACTUS FLAT   Hiko   Elgin
N. PK. MOKELUMNE   Lake Alpine   Mono Lake   Lee Vining   MONTGOMERY PK. 13441   WHITE MTN. PK. 14246   WHEELBARROW PK. 6420   Ash Springs   Alamo   Carp
Arnold   Dardanelle   Pinecrest   Bridgeport   June Lake   Benton   Lida   MAGRUDER MTN. 9046   Shivwits
Long Barn   YOSEMITE NATIONAL PARK   Mammoth Lakes   DEVILS POSTPILE NAT. MON.   Gold Point   Castle Cliff

G
37°
Tuolumne   Groveland   El Portal   Yosemite National Park   RED SLATE MTN. 13163   BISHOP IND. RES.   Laws   MT. HUMPHREYS 13986   Bishop   GRAPEVINE PK. 8738   SHOSHONE PK. 7056   MORMON PK. 7414   Mesquite   Bunkerville
Coulterville   Bagby   Cathay   Mariposa   Le Grand   Raymond   N. Fork   Big Creek   Friant   SPLIT MTN. 14058   KINGS CANYON NAT. PARK   Big Pine   Beatty   Lathrop Wells   DEATH VALLEY   Moapa   MOAPA RIVER IND. RES.   Overton   Logandale
Chowchilla   Madera   Fresno   Clovis   Tranquillity   Fowler   Auberry   Tollhouse   Dinkey Creek   MT. RITTER   KINGS CANYON NAT. PARK   Independence   MT. WHITNEY 14494   HIGHEST POINT IN CALIFORNIA   Lone Pine   Keeler   HAYFORD PK. 9912   SHEEP RANGE   Indian Springs   Las Vegas   Henderson
Selma   Kingsburg   Reedley   Dinuba   Sanger   SEQUOIA NAT. PARK   Death Valley   Cactus Spgs.   N. Las Vegas   NELLIS A.F.B.   Winchester   East Las Vegas   HOOVER DAM

H
36°
Helm   Lanare   Riverdale   Laton   Visalia   Hanford   Exeter   Woodlake   Lindsay   Strathmore   Porterville   OLANCHA PK. 12123   Olancha   Darwin   TELESCOPE PK. 11049   Pahrump   CHARLESTON PK. 11919   Paradise   Blue Diamond   Sloan   MT. WILSON 5445
Lemoore   Strafford   Tulare   Tipton   Pixley   Alpaugh   SIRRETTA PK. 9977   Johnsondale   282 FT. BELOW SEA LEVEL LOWEST POINT IN U.S.   Shoshone   Goodsprings   LAKE MEAD NATIONAL REC. AREA   Willow Bch.   HUALAPAI IND. RES.
Kettleman City   Corcoran   CHINA LAKE NAVAL WEAPONS CENTER   Tecopa   Jean   MC CULLOUGH MTS.   Boulder City   Searchlight
Avenal   TULE RIVER IND. RES.   BRECKINRIDGE MTN. 7580   Delano   McFarland   Kernville   Miracle Hot Springs   Trona   Westend   CHINA LAKE NAVAL WEAPONS CENTER   Nipton   Cima   Nelson   Cottonwood Cove   Searchlight   ARIZONA
Devils Den   Lost Hills   Wasco   Shafter   Oildale   Bakersfield   Caliente   Randsburg   Red Mountain   Baker   Laughlin   Kingman   HUALAPAI PK. 8417
McKittrick   Tupman   Lamont   Keene   Johannesburg   Searles L.   MOJAVE DESERT   DAVIS DAM   FT. MOJAVE IND. RES.   40
Taft   Ford City   Arvin   Tehachapi   Monolith   A-520529-71   COSMO SERIES NEVADA   RAND McNALLY & COMPANY   Longitude West of Greenwich
Maricopa   Mojave

35°
1 120°   2   119°   3   118°   4   117°   5   116°   6   115°   7   114°   8

WARNER MTS.   BLACK ROCK DESERT   HUMBOLDT   GREAT BASIN   SIERRA NEVADA   PAHUTE MESA   DEATH VALLEY NATIONAL MONUMENT   MOJAVE DESERT   SAN BERNARDINO   INYO

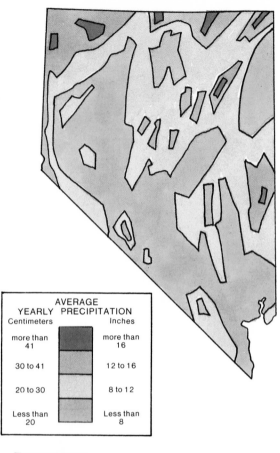

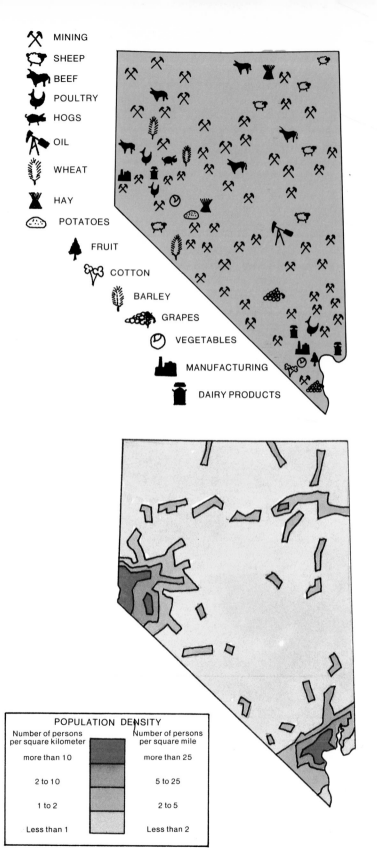

AVERAGE
YEARLY PRECIPITATION

Centimeters		Inches
more than 41		more than 16
30 to 41		12 to 16
20 to 30		8 to 12
Less than 20		Less than 8

MINING
SHEEP
BEEF
POULTRY
HOGS
OIL
WHEAT
HAY
POTATOES
FRUIT
COTTON
BARLEY
GRAPES
VEGETABLES
MANUFACTURING
DAIRY PRODUCTS

MAJOR
HIGHWAYS

POPULATION DENSITY

Number of persons per square kilometer		Number of persons per square mile
more than 10		more than 25
2 to 10		5 to 25
1 to 2		2 to 5
Less than 1		Less than 2

TOPOGRAPHY

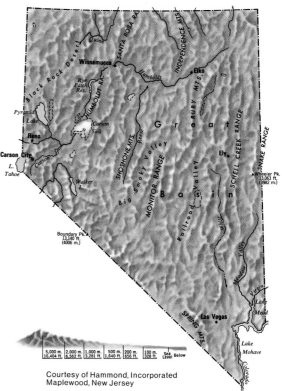

Winnemucca

Black Rock Desert

SANTA ROSA RANGE

INDEPENDENCE MTS.

Quinn

Humboldt

Elko

HUMBOLDT RA.

Rye
Patch
Res.

RUBY MTS.

SCHELL CREEK RANGE

SNAKE RANGE

Pyramid
Lake

Reno

Carson
Sink

G r e a t

SHOSHONE MTS.

Reese

Big Smoky Valley

MONITOR RANGE

Railroad Valley

Ely

Wheeler Pk.
13,063 ft.
(3982 m.)

Carson City

L.
Tahoe

Carson

Walker
L.

B a s i n

Boundary Pk.
13,140 ft.
(4006 m.)

White

Meadow Valley

Virgin

Lake
Mead

SPRING MTS.

Las Vegas

Lake
Mohave

Colorado

5,000 m. | 2,000 m. | 1,000 m. | 500 m. | 200 m. | 100 m. | Sea | Below
16,404 ft. | 6,562 ft. | 3,281 ft. | 1,640 ft. | 656 ft. | 328 ft. | Level

Courtesy of Hammond, Incorporated
Maplewood, New Jersey

COUNTIES

W A S H O E

HUMBOLDT

E L K O

Winnemucca

Elko

P E R S H I N G

Lovelock

L A N D E R

EUREKA

STOREY

Reno

CHURCHILL

Fallon

Austin

Eureka

WHITE PINE

Virginia City

CARSON CITY

ORMSBY

Ely

O

Minden

DOUGLAS

Yerington

Z

M I N E R A L

Hawthorne

Tonopah

N Y E

Pioche

ESMERALDA

Goldfield

L I N C O L N

C L A R K

Las Vegas

Reno's famous iron arch

INDEX

Page numbers that appear in boldface type indicate illustrations

138

A cattle drive in Carson Valley

Picture Identifications
Front cover: Brownstone and Red Rock canyons near Las Vegas
Back cover: Lake Tahoe
Pages 2-3: Pyramid Lake
Page 6: Lake Mead National Recreation Area
Pages 8-9: Cathedral Gorge State Park
Pages 18-19: Montage of Nevada residents
Page 24: Ancient petroglyphs at Lake Mead National Recreation Area
Page 36: Virginia City
Page 46: An early photograph of Goldfield
Page 58: Hoover Dam
Page 72: The dome of the Nevada State Capitol in Carson City
Pages 84-85: Skiers in the Ruby Mountains
Pages 94-95: Boundary Peak, Nevada's highest mountain
Page 108: Montage showing the state flag, state tree (single-leaf piñon), state animal (desert bighorn sheep), state flower (sagebrush), and state bird (mountain bluebird)

Picture Acknowledgments
Front cover, © **Kate Butler**; 2-3, © D. Muench/**H. Armstrong Roberts**; 4, © **Ed Cooper**; 5, © **Kate Butler**; 6, © D. Muench/**H. Armstrong Roberts**; 8-9, © Manley Photo/**SuperStock**; 11, © **Jay Aldrich**; 13 (left), © Stephen Trimble/**Root Resources**; 13 (right), 15 (left), © **Ed Cooper**; 15 (right), © D. Muench/**H. Armstrong Roberts**; 16 (left), © Ann Purcell/**Words and Pictures**; 16 (right), © **Kate Butler**; 18 (three photos), 19 (top left, bottom left), © **C. J. Hadley**; 19 (top right), © **Kate Butler**; 19 (bottom right), © **Jay Aldrich**; 21, © **Virginia R. Grimes**; 24, © Stephen Trimble/**Root Resources**; 26, © Mark E. Gibson/**Marilyn Gartman Agency**; 27 (left), **Historical Pictures Service, Chicago**; 27 (right), © **Eugene Jack**; 30 (left), © **Virginia R. Grimes**; 30 (right), **Nevada Historical Society**; 33, 35, **Historical Pictures Service, Chicago**; 36, © Ed Cooper/**H. Armstrong Roberts**; 39, **Courtesy, The Bancroft Library**; 40, **The Thomas Gilcrease Institute of American History and Art, Tulsa, Oklahoma**; 43, **Historical Pictures Service, Chicago**; 44 (two photos), 46, **Nevada Historical Society**; 48 (left), © **Virginia R. Grimes**; 48 (right), **Nevada Historical Society**; 49 (left), © **Larry Prosor**; 49 (right), **Nevada Historical Society**; 50 (left), © **Jay Aldrich**; 50 (right), **North Wind Picture Archives**; 53, 54, **Nevada Historical Society**; 57, **AP/Wide World Photos**; 58, © Dave Brown/**Journalism Services**; 60, **Nevada Historical Society**; 63, © **Larry Prosor**; 64 (left), © Audrey Gibson/**Marilyn Gartman Agency**; 64 (right), **The Bettmann Archive**; 65, 67 (left), **AP/Wide World Photos**; 67 (right), **Photri**; 68, **Historical Pictures Service, Chicago**; 71, **AP/Wide World Photos**; 72, © **Jay Aldrich**; 75 (left), © **Virginia R. Grimes**; 75 (right), © R. Krubner/**H. Armstrong Roberts**; 76 (left), © **Jay Aldrich**; 76 (right), © Carl Purcell/**Words and Pictures**; 77 (top left), © John Cancalosi/**Tom Stack & Associates**; 77 (bottom left), **Nevada Commission of Tourism**; 77 (right), © **Bob Goodman**; 78, © Ann Duncan/**Tom Stack & Associates**; 79, © Linda Dufurrena/**Tom Stack & Associates**; 80, © **Jay Aldrich**; 81, © **Kate Butler**; 84-85, © **Larry Prosor**; 87 (two photos), © **Jay Aldrich**; 88 (two photos), © **Eugene Jack**; 89 (left), © Carl Purcell/**Words and Pictures**; 89 (right), © Mark E. Gibson/**Marilyn Gartman Agency**; 90, © **Ed Cooper**; 91 (two photos), © Brian Parker/**Tom Stack & Associates**; 93, © **Larry Prosor**; 94-95, 97, © **Ed Cooper**; 97 (map), **Len W. Meents**; 99 (two photos), © **Larry Prosor**; 99 (map), **Len W. Meents**; 100, © Linda Dufurrena/**Tom Stack & Associates**; 102 (two photos), © **Ed Cooper**; 105, © J. Blank/**H. Armstrong Roberts**; 106, © **Kate Butler**; 106 (map), **Len W. Meents**; 108 (tree), © Kenneth W. Fink/**Root Resources**; 108 (bird), © Anthony Mercieca/**Root Resources**; 108 (bighorn sheep), © Thomas Kitchin/**Tom Stack & Associates**; 108 (sagebrush), © Eric Carle/**SuperStock**; 108 (flag), **Courtesy Flag Research Center, Winchester, Massachusetts 01890**; 111, © Clive Friend/**SuperStock**; 112, © **Larry Prosor**; 113, © Thomas Styczynski/**TSW-Click/Chicago Ltd.**; 114 (left), © **Ed Cooper**; 114 (right), © Bill Everitt/**Tom Stack & Associates**; 115 (left), © **Lynn M. Stone**; 115 (right), © **Bob Goodman**; 116, © **Ed Cooper**; 118, © **C. J. Hadley**; 120, © Jay Aldrich; 121, © **Ed Cooper**; 122, © **C. J. Hadley**; 125, **Nevada Historical Society**; 126, **H. Armstrong Roberts**; 127, 128 (Clemens, Clark), **AP/Wide World Photos**; 128 (Dat-So-La-Lee), **Nevada State Museum**; 128 (Fair), **Historical Pictures Service, Chicago**; 129 (Frémont), **AP/Wide World Photos**; 129 (Hopkins), **Nevada Historical Society**; 129 (Liberace, Mackay), 130 (Nevada, Newlands), **Historical Pictures Service, Chicago**; 130 (Oddie, Pittman), 131 (Russell, Sobers), **AP/Wide World Photos**; 131 (Stewart, Sutro), **Historical Pictures Service, Chicago**; 132 (Vucanovich), **AP/Wide World Photos**; 132 (Wovoka), **Historical Pictures Service, Chicago**; 136 (maps), **Len W. Meents**; 138, © **Ed Cooper**; 141, © **Jay Aldrich**; back cover, © **Ed Cooper**

About the Authors

Dee Lillegard was born and raised in California and has traveled extensively throughout the neighboring state of Nevada. Ms. Lillegard has written numerous books for young people, including several titles for Childrens Press.

Wayne McMurray Stoker was born in Alabama, but has spent most of his life in California. For many years, Mr. Stoker has explored the back roads and ghost towns of Nevada. He is currently at work on a young-adult novel set in Nevada's high desert.

144